PROTECTING YOUR COMMISSIONS

A Sales Representative's Guide

Randall J. Gillary

 R.J. Law Publishing • Troy, Michigan

Protecting Your Commissions
A Sales Representative's Guide
By Randall J. Gillary

Published by:
R.J. Law Publishing, L.L.C.
201 West Big Beaver Rd., Ste. 1020
Troy, MI 48084 U.S.A.
http://www.gillarylaw.com

ISBN, print ed.   0-9741847-0-5
Printed in the United States of America

Library of Congress Cataloging-in-Publication Data

Gillary, Randall J.
Protecting Your Commissions—A Sales Representative's Guide
ISBN: 0-9741847-0-5
Library of Congress Catalog Card Number: 2003-107640

DEDICATION

This book is dedicated to my daughter Kimberly who was with us for only fifteen and a half short years. She taught me more than I could ever explain about life, love, and faith. I will miss her and love her every day of my life.

http://www.gillarylaw.com

TABLE OF CONTENTS

Chapter 3:
YOU HAVE AN AGREEMENT – NOW WHAT DO YOU DO?   71

Chapter 4:
SPECIAL CONSIDERATIONS   91

Chapter 5:
BE AWARE: FOREWARNED IS FOREARMED   101

Chapter 6:
TERMINATION   111

Chapter 7:
LITIGATING YOUR COMMISSION DISPUTE   143

PROLOGUE

My name is Randall J. Gillary
and I live in Troy, Michigan.
I have been a practicing
attorney for twenty-four
years. I have spent most of
my career representing
manufacturer's
representatives and other
salespeople in commission
disputes.

I consider myself to be an advocate for salespeople. I
decided to take some of my experiences over the past
twenty years and put them into somewhat of a handbook
form. My purpose is to help salespeople to deal with the
types of problems which they will experience in their
day-to-day relationships with their employers
/principals.

An important caveat to keep in mind is that this book is
not intended to be a substitute for competent legal
advice. For the most part, I will be addressing issues in a
general manner. Additionally, and most importantly,
law and legal principles can vary significantly from state
to state. Your individual problems will need to be
individually addressed. This book is intended to
supplement your relationship with your lawyer, not to be
used in lieu of competent legal advice. Remember, you
get what you pay for.

One of the truisms which one learns as a salesperson is that achieving success in the sales field is often a double-edged sword. The more successful you are, the more money you are generally paid, and the more vulnerable you therefore become. Large commission checks often equate to stress in your relationship with your principal or employer. One would think that this should not be a problem but it often is. You will find that many principals/employers have a very difficult time writing large commission checks. Part of this is human nature. Greed and envy have been with us longer than recorded history, and I doubt that it will change in our lifetimes. I often say that human nature is my job security.

I am a member of the Detroit Golf Club and had dinner there one evening with a friend of mine, Jim Edwards, who is a highly successful business owner. We had just finished a team match in our Tuesday evening golf league. We happened to be talking about my law practice and commission disputes. Jim indicated to me that there was nothing he would rather do than write large commission checks. Large commission payments mean that he is making money. I told him that if everyone thought the way he did, I would be out of a job. You will find that there are many principals or owners who think the way my friend does, but many more, it seems, who do not. It is for those salespersons who have to deal with the latter that this book is written.

Even if you are one of those persons lucky enough to work for an employer or principal who thinks like my friend, you must expect that at some point in time your situation will change. Ownership of companies can change, and what was once a very good relationship can turn sour very quickly. I have seen it happen. Hopefully, by reading this book you will be able to anticipate some of the problems which can occur and be in a position to appropriately deal with them. In any business, one of the keys to success is being able to anticipate problems and to plan for negative consequences. The time to prepare yourself is when things are going well.

In the mid-seventies while I was in law school, I read a book entitled *Looking Out for Number One*.[1] This is an excellent book written by Robert Ringer. One of the key points of the book is that you can achieve positive results by assuming negative things will happen. It is somewhat of a corollary to Murphy's Law. It is always important to remember that if anything can go wrong, it will, and usually at the worst possible time. By following these principles, you will be better prepared for the bad things which will happen. The purpose of this book is to help you to anticipate the problems which you will experience in your life as a salesperson and to help you to have a plan to deal with those problems.

The organization of this book is set up to follow the course of a typical sales representation relationship. I begin with the formation of your relationship with your principal or employer and conclude with litigating a commission dispute. In between, I address typical problems which you can expect to experience with your employer or principal during the course of your

---

[1] Fawcett Crest, New York

relationship. At times, I will be discussing some of the specific cases in which I have been involved. In some instances, I will use the real names of the parties. In other instances, where we have settled cases and have signed confidentiality agreements, I will address some of the issues in more general terms in accordance with the agreements which have been signed. More than just war stories, these cases will hopefully have the effect of illustrating with live examples some of the points which I make in this book.

Much of the information and advice which is included in these pages has been published previously in other forms. I have written several articles which have been published in *Agency Sales Magazine*. *Agency Sales Magazine* is a marketing magazine for manufacturer's sales agencies and their principals. It is published by the Manufacturer's Agents National Association (MANA), based in Laguna Hills, California. MANA is an excellent organization supporting manufacturer's representatives and principals. A listing of the articles is included at the end of this book. The purpose of the articles has always been to help salespeople in dealing with some of their day-to-day problems. It has been my belief that if I can help to educate salespeople they will be in a better position to avoid legal problems. Their sales representation relationships with their employers or principals should then run more smoothly.

I have also written or co-authored two legal articles. The first was *The History Of The Procuring Cause Doctrine In Michigan*, 74 Mich. B.J. 1264 (1995). The second article was co-authored by my Associate, Kevin P. Albus, and is entitled *Michigan's Sales Representative Act Revisited - Again - Or, Does "Intentionally" Mean "In Bad Faith?"*, 2001 L. REV. M.S.U.-D.C.L. 965. These articles were written primarily for lawyers and address my view of sales representative law in the State of Michigan on specific topics.

My goal in my law practice is to do whatever I can, consistent with the Rules of Professional Conduct, to obtain a winning result for my clients. Sometimes this means avoiding a lawsuit. In other cases it may mean negotiating a settlement or trying a case in front of a judge, jury, or arbitration panel. Whichever way a problem is solved, I always try to remember that the practice of law is a service business. Frankly, I have taken some criticism from some of my competitors who believe I am "giving all of the secrets away". I try, however, to run my business like most salespeople do. Generally, you will be successful in the sales business if you make solving your customer's problem your first priority. A customer frankly, isn't too interested whether you are going to make any money or not. He is more interested in having you solve his problem. Whether it is the design or manufacturing of a new part, improving a production process, or merely supplying widgets, successful salespeople make their customers' satisfaction their number one priority. If a salesperson is successful in that goal, the economic benefits will generally follow.

I try to run my law practice in the same way. If I can solve my clients' problems and obtain a positive result, the economic benefits will follow. Too many lawyers make the maximization of their legal fees their number one priority, rather than solving their clients' problems. This is one reason why the legal profession has an image problem. Lawyers can often be their own worst enemies. If we as lawyers remembered that our charge is to help people, we would generally be better respected.

This book is not intended to be read once and then discarded. Hopefully you will be able to use it as a resource guide to refer to throughout your sales career. Please remember that this book is not intended to provide legal advice. Legal advice should be given by your own lawyer who has carefully evaluated your legal problem.

I would like to point out that if you read this book carefully, you will find some inconsistencies. Part of the reason for this is that the practice of law is more an art than a science. Legal advice is predicated upon many factors and can vary significantly based upon individual circumstances. The personalities of the players, their relative economic power, the situs of any litigation, and many other factors can significantly influence the strategic advice given by a lawyer. Human dynamics can be a significant factor in deciding the best course of action to take. You must remember that legal disputes are ultimately resolved by judges, juries, or arbitrators, i.e., people. Reasonable arguments can almost always be made on either side of an issue. The advice given to one client under one set of circumstances does not necessarily apply to a different client under very similar circumstances. This is one of the great challenges of the practice of law. A good lawyer has to be part scientist, part psychologist, part statistician, part soothsayer, part philosopher, and part warrior. Try to find a good lawyer who you can talk to, work with, and trust. If you do find a good lawyer, try to hang onto him or her throughout your career.

Randy Gillary
July, 2003

1

The Formation of Your Sales Representative Agreement

Go Straight to the Heart of Danger

In my freshman English Literature course at the University of Michigan in 1969, one of our assignments was to read the book entitled *Heart of Danger*, by Harold Pease.[1] In the beginning of the book was an old Chinese proverb which I try to follow in my business and personal life: "Go straight to the heart of danger, for there you will find peace." As a manufacturer's representative, when negotiating with your principal, or in any other aspect of your business, you should confront your problems and issues head-on. Don't be afraid to address the tough topics. In the beginning stages of your manufacturer's representative agreement, you should be able to make the case for a reasonable post-termination commission payout. In the automotive industry, for example, you may be working for two or three years without compensation before you will have the opportunity to acquire any new business. It is only fair that you receive a reasonable post-termination

---

[1]Out of print.

commission payout to compensate you adequately for your time.

If your principal is not willing to agree with you on this, you may be better off looking for a different principal to represent. You must assume that your principal will always act in its own economic self-interest. In many cases, this will mean terminating you after you have been responsible for procuring a large order in order to avoid paying the commissions. Believe me, this does happen. You should always try to avoid a circumstance in which your principal has an economic incentive to terminate you. Address these issues as soon as possible in the relationship whenever you can.

Written or Oral Agreement: Which Is Better?

As a general rule, the answer to this question would appear to be self-evident. Most people would agree that sales representation agreements and other commission arrangements should be in writing.[2] I also subscribe to this philosophy. There are certain circumstances, however, where less is more.

Generally, the best possible protection you can have is for your lawyer to prepare a sales representation agreement or commission plan and to have it signed by your

---

[2] The states of Arkansas, California, Florida, New Hampshire, New York, Pennsylvania, Virginia, and Washington have statutes requiring contracts with sales representatives to be in writing.

principal or employer.[3] You should also be sure that your lawyer is experienced in sales representation law and understands your business. My principal objective in representing my clients is to try to ensure that they get paid for the business which they generate for their employers or principals. Generally, the best possible protection is a well-written contract which describes the circumstances under which you will be paid. At the top of the hierarchy, in terms of protection, is a written contract drafted by your attorney who understands sales law and your business. Such a contract should provide security that you will be paid a commission for all business which you are responsible for generating for your employer or principal, regardless of termination.

Since I live and work in Michigan where the automotive industry is the dominant industry, much of my practice is automotive industry–related. This creates a unique set of circumstances which are often not present in other industries. Many automotive salespeople, whether they are independent manufacturer's representatives or employee salespersons, are primarily involved in selling production parts or related products.

---

[3] As a practical matter, you may often have very little input into your sales representation agreement or commission plan. Many manufacturer's representatives are given form contracts and told to sign them "as is" if they want to represent the manufacturer or handle the line. Most employee salespeople have very little input into their compensation plans. Management generally prepares the plan and submits it to the salesperson without any room for negotiation.

The typical life of an automotive "platform"[4] is five to seven years. It can be ten years or more for trucks. A salesperson who is selling automotive production parts is primarily responsible for making sure that the parts are included on a particular vehicle. Generally, the automotive industry is working two or three model years in advance and sometimes more. This means that a salesperson today will be attempting to "sell a part" for which production may not even commence for three to four years. If the automotive customer issues a purchase order for the particular part, then the part can be in production for up to five to seven years for automotive parts and up to ten years for truck parts.

The objective in negotiating a sales representation agreement, if you are an automotive sales representative, is to ensure that you are paid a commission for the life of part or product if possible. A written contract which provides that, in event of termination, the salesperson will be paid a commission for the life of part or the life of the product will put the salesperson in the strongest legal position. Obtaining such a contract is easier said than done, however. Many principals will not agree to this. Further, at the commencement of the relationship, it is sometimes difficult to engage in extended discussions about what will happen when the relationship terminates. It is similar to negotiating and signing a prenuptial agreement with your fiancée addressing how the marital property will be distributed in the event of a divorce. Sometimes this can be easily addressed and at other times it can be a very difficult subject to discuss.

---

[4] A "platform" is typically a vehicle chassis.

You must keep in mind that your principal economic objective as a salesperson, whether you are an independent salesperson or an employee, is to maximize the dollars in your pocket. There is a difference between an established sales agency, which can insist upon a "life of part" provision in the sales representation agreement, and a novice, who needs the principal or employer to put food on the table. In many instances, there are sacrifices that need to be made in order to generate income, and "life of part" commissions is often one of them. Unfortunately, this can be a fact of life in the sales business.

In negotiating your sales representation agreement, or in negotiating anything, you must remember two key principles. The first is to have a clear understanding of the relative strength of your bargaining position. Are you the highly sought-after salesperson or sales agency already well-entrenched in the marketplace, so that the principal or employer needs you more than you need them? If so, you can be aggressive in negotiating the best possible representation agreement. If you are the novice in dire need of a product line or a job, you may have to be less choosy. Be realistic about where in that spectrum you are.

The second key principle is that whatever position you are in, you should make the most of it. Whether you are the novice or experienced professional, try to make the best possible deal you can under the circumstances. Getting back to the question posed at the beginning of this chapter, there are circumstances under which an oral or handshake agreement can be better than a written agreement. In the automotive industry, for example, you may be better off without a written agreement if you are not able to negotiate an acceptable post-termination commission payout.

In Michigan, as in many other states, sales representatives may be protected by the Procuring Cause Doctrine.[5] Under this doctrine, a salesperson may be entitled to a commission if he[6] was the procuring cause of a sale, notwithstanding that he has been terminated. It is difficult to define precisely what "procuring cause" means. The Michigan Supreme Court has defined "procuring cause" as the "chief means by which [a] sale was finally effected."[7] Under some circumstances, it is possible to pursue a "life of part" commission claim in the absence of a written contract. I will often advise my clients that they may be better off with no written agreement whatsoever addressing the issue of termination commissions. This is generally true in the instances in which my client believes his principal will not agree to pay any significant post-termination commissions. If there is no express agreement limiting post-termination commissions, then a salesperson may

---

[5] Please see Gillary, *The History Of The Procuring Cause Doctrine In Michigan*, 74 MICH. B.J. 1264 (1995).

[6] Although I recognize that many salespeople are women (many of my clients have been women), I have used the masculine gender throughout this book in referring to sales representatives and their principals for simplicity purposes.

[7] Kinsey v. Barth, 158 NW 872 (Mich. 1916), quoting with approval the trial court's instructions to the jury.

have the ability to argue commissions for "life of part" in the event of a termination.

Whether or not you are successful in a lawsuit will generally depend upon the circumstances. Ordinarily, if the salesperson is the procuring cause of the initial purchase order, we can make a good argument for "life of part" commissions in Michigan. Keep in mind, however, that many states do not following the Procuring Cause Doctrine. In many cases you may need an express contractual provision in order to receive post-termination commissions. Be sure to review this issue with your lawyer.

If my client does not believe he will be able to negotiate an acceptable post-termination provision, then I sometimes recommend a simple letter agreement or even a confirming letter. In the hierarchy of contracts, a letter agreement signed by the principal or employer and the salesperson is generally next on the list. A typical letter agreement could be as follows:

Sample Letter

ABC Manufacturing Company
Anywhere, U.S.A

Attn: President

Re: Sales Representation Agreement

Dear President:

This is to confirm that XYZ Sales Agency will be the exclusive sales representative for ABC Manufacturing Company to (identify the specific accounts or specific territory) for the sale of the (describe product) manufactured or supplied by ABC Manufacturing Company. It is understood that the XYZ Sales Agency will be paid a commission at the rate of X% for all sales which we are able to generate for life of the part or program.

We look forward to a long and mutually beneficial relationship.

Sincerely,

Expert Salesperson,
XYZ Sales Agency

_____

Agreed:

_____

President, ABC Manufacturing Company

Such a letter agreement can give the salesperson a claim for "life of part" commissions.

The next level down in the hierarchy of effective sales agreements would be essentially the same letter, but without the signature of the president of the manufacturing company. If there is no contrary correspondence disputing the terms of the letter, then this can be used to demonstrate that the letter represents the agreement.

If you believe that your principal will not agree to a "life of part" provision in a letter agreement, another option would be to have the letter state that you as the sales representative will be paid a commission for all sales which you are responsible for generating. As indicated earlier, as long as there is no express agreement limiting commissions in the event of a termination you may be able to assert a claim for "life of part" commissions pursuant to the Procuring Cause Doctrine in Michigan. A sample confirming letter is as follows:

Sample Letter

ABC Manufacturing Company
Anywhere, U.S.A.

Attn: President

Re: Sales Representation Agreement

Dear President:

This is to confirm that XYZ Sales Agency will be the exclusive sales representative for ABC Manufacturing Company to (identify the specific accounts or specific territory) for the sale of (describe product) manufactured or supplied by ABC Manufacturing Company. It is understood that XYZ Sales Agency will be paid a commission at the rate of X% for all sales which we are responsible for procuring.

We look forward to a long and mutually beneficial relationship.

Sincerely,

Expert Salesperson
XYZ Sales Agency

In summary, the hierarchy of effective sales representation agreements is as follows:

1.   Expertly written sales representation agreement with "life of part" or "life of the program" termination provision;

2.   Letter agreement with "life of part" termination provision signed by the principal;

3.   Confirming letter that commissions will be paid for the life of part or program;

4.   Letter agreement providing that a commission will be paid for all sales generated by the salesperson;

5.   Confirming letter that a commission will be paid for all sales generated by the salesperson;

6.   Oral agreement.

The obvious fact issue in the event of a termination and litigation is "What sales was the salesperson responsible for generating or procuring?" Generally, you want to avoid anything in writing which specifically limits the commissions in the event of your termination.[8]

---

[8] Historically this has been true in Michigan, but there is a relatively recent Court of Appeals decision which seems to hold to the contrary. The case is *Walters v. Bloomfield Hills Furniture*, 577 NW2d 206 (Mich. 1998). In the *Walters* case, the Court of Appeals overturned a trial court decision. The trial court decision dismissed a salesperson's

One key disadvantage of an oral agreement or a letter agreement is the difficulty of obtaining commissions in the event of the sale of the assets or business of the principal. This can be a major problem which will be addressed in more detail in Chapter Six. I would highly recommend that you review that section before utilizing a letter agreement.

Employee Compensation/Commission Plans and the Law of Unilateral Contracts

This section is primarily intended to apply to employee salespersons who are provided with a written commission plan or a compensation agreement. There is a distinction between employee commission plans and

---

claim for commissions on furniture delivered after the plaintiff's termination of employment based upon a written acknowledgment that no commissions would be paid for furniture delivered after termination. The written acknowledgment was signed well after the commencement of the employment and modified the prior oral agreement between the plaintiff and the company.

The Court of Appeals ruled that the written acknowledgment was unenforceable because it violated the Michigan Sales Representatives Commission Act. The purpose of the act is to protect a salesperson's entitlement to commissions on sales made during the course of his employment. Notwithstanding the *Walters* case, you should avoid signing any documents which unfairly restrict your commissions in the event of a termination.

bonus arrangements. Generally, commission plans are based upon objective sales criteria. In Michigan, a commission is defined as "... compensation accruing to a sales representative for payment by a principal, the rate of which is expressed as a percentage of the amount of orders or sales or as a percentage of the dollar amount of profits." (MCL 600.2961 (1)(a)). Bonus plans often use components which are discretionary. Bonuses may not result in a contractual entitlement because of their subjective nature. Generally, an objective commission plan is legally enforceable. A subjective or discretionary bonus plan may not be.

We have handled several commission disputes for employee salespersons in which there were significant changes to the commission plans or compensation agreements prior to the end of a plan year/fiscal year. These generally involved circumstances in which the salesperson substantially exceeded sales projections or other expectations. The problem often arises when the commission payment will result in the salesperson making more than upper management believes the position is generally worth. One such case is *Sharon Holland v. Earl Graves Publishing Company*. This decision is reported at *Holland v. Earl G. Graves Publishing Co.*, 46 F. Supp. 2d 681 (E.D. Mich. 1998).

Sharon Holland was a salesperson for *Black Enterprise Magazine*. She was provided with a compensation plan which generally provided that she would be paid a commission based upon the advertising revenue from her main accounts. One of her key accounts was General Motors Corporation. Sharon Holland was in a unique position because she had grown up in the metropolitan Detroit area and knew many of the key General Motors personnel. In part based upon Sharon's personal contacts, she was able to determine that *Black Enterprise Magazine* could substantially increase its advertising revenue if it would enter into an agreement with General Motors Media Works. The agreement, in essence, would provide for a quantity discount. Sharon made arrangements for her boss, Mr. Earl G. Graves, Jr., to come to Detroit to meet with key General Motors personnel. The meeting resulted in a contract being entered into between *Black Enterprise Magazine* and General Motors Corporation which substantially increased advertising revenue for *Black Enterprise Magazine*.

At the conclusion of the fiscal year for the compensation plan, Sharon earned a bonus of $98,285. After the fiscal year had ended, Sharon was called to New York for a meeting with Mr. Earl Graves, Jr. In that meeting, he indicated to her that her quota was being increased by $250,000. In essence, Mr. Graves, Jr., took credit for the increased General Motors business and reduced Sharon's commission by $55,000. Needless to say, Sharon was quite upset. She stayed employed with *Black Enterprise Magazine* for approximately another year until she was able to, ironically, obtain a job with General Motors Corporation. We then filed a lawsuit on Sharon's behalf in Michigan. United States District Judge Paul V. Gadola granted our motion for summary judgment and ruled that *Black Enterprise Magazine* could not retroactively

increase Sharon's quota after she had already performed.
We recovered her entire commission plus interest.[9]

The *Holland* v *Graves* decision is significant because it was
the first reported decision interpreting Michigan law
holding that employee commission plans can constitute
an offer for a unilateral contract.[10] In his Memorandum
Opinion and Order Granting Plaintiff's Renewed Motion
for Summary Judgment, Judge Gadola wrote as follows:

> The formation of a unilateral contract typically
> involves a case in which an offer is made by a
> party which invites acceptance by performance
> rather than by a promise to perform.
> *Restatement (Second) of Contracts,* § 45, cmt. a
> (1979). *See also* A. Farnsworth, *Contracts* § 3.4
> (2d ed. 1990); 1 Arthur L. Corbin, *Corbin on
> Contracts* § 70 (1963). Once an offer for a
> unilateral contract is made, and part of the
> requested performance has been rendered by
> the offeree, the offer cannot be unilaterally
> revoked or modified. *Restatement (Second) of
> Contracts* §§ 25, 45 & cmt. d (1981); 1 Corbin,

---

[9] We were not able to recover any penalties under
the Michigan Sales Commission Act because Sharon sold
advertising services. Judge Gadola ruled that the Michigan
Sales Commission Act applied to the sale of goods and that
advertising services were not covered.

[10] There had been prior Michigan decisions applying
unilateral contract principles to severance plans. See, e.g.,
Cain v. Allen Electric & Equipment Co., 78 NW2d 296 (Mich.
1956) and *Gaydos v. White Motor Co.,* 220 NW2d 697 (Mich.
1974).

Contracts § 63 (1952); 1 *Williston on Contracts* (rev. ed. 1990) § 5:13, 691.692.

Corbin on Contracts sets forth the following discussion of unilateral contracts with regard to bonus programs offered by employers, which is particularly relevant in this case.

'The same unilateral contract analysis is applicable to the employer's promise to pay a bonus or pension to an employee in case the latter continues to serve for a stated period. It is now recognized that these are not pure gratuities but compensation for services rendered. The employer's promise is not enforceable when made, but the employee can accept the offer by continuing to serve as requested, even though the employee makes no promise. There is no mutuality of obligation, but there is consideration in the form of service rendered. The employee's one consideration, rendition of services, supports all of the employer's promises, to pay the salary and to pay the bonus. Indeed, although the bonus is not fully earned until the service has continued for the full time, after a substantial part of the service has been rendered the offer of the bonus cannot be withdrawn without a breach of contract.'

2 Corbin, *Contracts* §6.2 (ref. ed. 1995).

Michigan courts have applied the theory of 'unilateral contracts' in a number of cases involving job benefits. For instance, in *Cain v. Allen Electric & Equipment Co.*, 346 Mich. 568, 78 N.W.2d 296 (1956), the court found that a personnel policy containing a severance pay provision presented an offer for a unilateral contract. The court stated, '[t]he essence of the announcement was precisely that the company would conduct itself in a certain way with the stated objective of achieving fairness, and we would be reluctant to hold under such circumstances that an employee might not reasonably rely on the expression made and conduct himself accordingly.' *Id.* at 579, 78 N.W.2d 296. The court further stated:

'In short, the adoption of the described policies by the company [regarding severance pay] constituted an offer of contract. This offer, as the trial court correctly held, 'the plaintiff accepted * * * by continuing in its employment beyond the 5-year period specified in exhibit B (the termination pay policy).' The offer having thus been accepted it was not within defendant's power to withdraw it when called upon to perform. The 'change or amendment to which the company policy was said, in its preamble, to be subject, could not encompass denial of a contract right gained through acceptance of an offer.'

Id. at 579-80, 78 NW2d 296.

Likewise in *Gaydos v. White Motor Corp.*, 54 Mich. App. 143, 220 N.W.2d 697 (1974), the Michigan Court of Appeals found a severance pay policy constituted an offer of contract and not a mere gratuity. *Id.* at 148, 220 N.W.2d 697. The court stated that "[a]s the employees continued to work [after the policy was established], consideration was supplied for a unilateral contract, upon which the employees had the right to rely." *Id.* See also *Clarke v. Brunswick Corp.*, 48 Mich. App. 667, 211 N.W.2d 101 (1973) (holding that a severance pay policy was a unilateral contract); *Couch v. Difco Lab. Inc.*, 44 Mich. App. 33 (1972) (finding that by establishing a profit-sharing plan, defendant-company offered to make certain payments for the benefit of its salaried employees who continued to render their services).

This court finds that, similar to the severance pay policies in *Caine* and *Gaydos*, the 1994/1995 compensation agreement was an offer for a unilateral contract. It was an announcement as to the way the company would conduct itself, and it could be accepted only by the plaintiff's performance. *Cain*, 346 Mich. at 579, 78 N.W.2d 296. The 1994/1995 compensation agreement stated in part:

'This Fiscal Year End Volume Incentive Plan will reward you if you generate net revenue above your annual quota, and will be paid based on an escalating percentage of net revenue above your annual quota. The percentage breakdown is as follows: . . .'

Having found that an offer for a unilateral contract was made in the 1994/1995 compensation package, the question thus becomes whether defendant could modify it without the mutual assent of both parties after plaintiff began substantially performing under the 1994/1995 compensation package. This court finds that it could not. *Cain* and *Gaydos* make that clear.

> The alteration to plaintiff's quota was most
> certainly a modification. There is no provision
> in the 1994/1995 compensation agreement
> which provides for such a modification.
> *Holland, supra* at 685-687.

Essentially Judge Gadola was stating that a binding contract was created by *Black Enterprise Magazine's* issuance of the compensation plan which was accepted by Sharon Holland through the rendition of her services in securing the new advertising business from General Motors. This offer and acceptance created a binding contract between Sharon Holland and *Black Enterprise Magazine*. *Black Enterprise Magazine* breached the contract when it failed to pay Sharon Holland her commission of $54,550.

Judge Gadola then went on to address a key issue in his opinion concerning the issue of consent by the employee. This is of major importance to any employee who is about to have a compensation change imposed upon him by his employer. *Consent to the change can eliminate any ability to later attempt to contest the change.*

> Having found that defendant clearly modified
> the unilateral offer when it changed her quota,
> the follow-up question is whether plaintiff
> assented to the modification. There is no
> evidence in the record that plaintiff ever
> assented to such a modification. Assuming for
> the sake of argument that plaintiff was
> presented with her quota change in February
> 1995, the fact that she remained at the
> defendant company for over one year after
> learning of the quota change is not, in this

court's eyes, evidence of her assent. *Farrell v. Automobile Club of Michigan*, 187 Mich. App. 220, 228, 466 N.W.2d 298 (1990) (rejecting the argument that acceptance of an offer for a modification to an employment contract can be presumed from the mere fact of continued employment and noting that such an offer could never be rejected absent one leaving employment).

In sum, the 1994/1995 compensation agreement contained a unilateral offer that plaintiff would receive a fiscal year end volume incentive award of 20% of the amount her net revenue exceeded her net revenue quota of $1,342,000. Once plaintiff began substantially performing, that offer could not be modified without plaintiff's assent. Here, the uncontroverted evidence is that plaintiff's quota was changed without any assent by her to the same. Thus, as a matter of law this court finds that defendant breached a contract with the plaintiff. Judgment should be entered in favor of the plaintiff for $54,550, the difference between the amount she was paid as a year-end volume incentive award and the amount she should have been paid under the terms of the 1994/1995 compensation package as originally presented to her. Plaintiff is also entitled to interest at the statutory rate. *Holland, supra* at 687.

The lesson to be learned here is that you must not agree to a retroactive adjustment in your quota or any other disadvantageous change in your compensation plan. You are in a stronger position if you are able to document

your objections to the proposed change. In Sharon
Holland's case, she was silent regarding whether she
accepted or rejected the change. Silence ordinarily is not
considered to be acceptance. This can be a significant
dilemma for you if your employer or principal makes
changes in your compensation or commission plan. If
you vehemently object, then you may be terminated. If
you do not object, then you may or may not be able to
later raise objections depending upon the circumstances.
If you receive benefits from the change, then it will be
much more difficult to go back and contest the change at
a later time. In Sharon Holland's case, she received no
benefit--only a detriment in the form of a reduced
commission payment. The court found in this case that
her silence was not acceptance.

Commission Plans Which State That the Plan Can Be Changed at Any Time

I have had several clients who are employee salespersons
with commission plans which include language stating
that the commission plan can be changed or modified at
any time. This does *not* necessarily mean that the plan
can be changed or modified at any time and for any
reason.[11] I generally take the position that the plan can be

---

[11] As noted by Judge Gadola on page 17, quoting the
Michigan Supreme Court in *Cain v. Allen Electric*, "The
'change' or amendment to which the company policy was
said, in its preamble, to be subject, could not encompass
denial of a contract right gained through acceptance of an
offer."

changed prospectively, i.e., for new orders or projects being solicited after the effective date of the change. A plan cannot generally be changed retroactively, however, i.e., for orders or projects that were solicited under the old plan. This would be a violation of the unilateral contract. Whether this argument is successful or not depends on several factors. These include:

1.   The extent of the progress on the project or order under the prior plan

2.   The specific language of the plan

3.   The reason for the change

4.   Whether the salesperson objected to the change or agreed or acquiesced to it

Commission plans are a matter of contract. If you do not object to attempts to reduce your commissions, then you may have difficulty challenging such a change. As indicated by Judge Gadola in *Holland v Graves*, after it was determined that the defendant modified the commission plan/unilateral offer when it changed the quota, "...the follow-up question is whether plaintiff assented to the modification."

I recently handled a case in which a commission plan was changed eleven months into the plan year, involving the sale of a new information handling system for a health care system and series of hospitals. The total package, including licensing fees, software, and hardware, was approximately $36 million. After the project had been quoted and it was reasonably certain my client's company would be awarded the business, the commission plan was changed and a cap on commissionable margin was unilaterally instituted. Prior to the change, there was no cap. This change had the effect of reducing my client's commissions by approximately $350,000. Unfortunately, my client signed a copy of the new commission plan. The trial judge ruled that the signature on the new plan constituted a consent to the change and granted a summary judgment in favor of the employer. My client decided not to appeal.

The salesperson would have been in a substantially stronger legal position if he had refused to sign the new plan. Although this would likely have resulted in an immediate termination, he was terminated shortly after signing the new plan anyway. My client was quite vocal in his disapproval of the fact that the plan was changed, depriving him of approximately $350,000 in commissions. No employer wants an employee who strongly believes that he was treated unfairly to the extent of $350,000.

If this is about to happen to you, *do not sign the new plan before you obtain competent legal advice from an attorney familiar with the law of unilateral contracts. If you do sign, you must assume the new plan will govern and will be enforceable.* If you do not sign, you will likely be terminated, but this may be inevitable anyway. Most salespeople do not want to work for an employer who treats them unfairly.

If no signature is required on the plan, you should object in writing. Otherwise, your continued employment without objection can be considered consent.[12] You should deal with the issue immediately and directly. Sometimes you can work out an accommodation and sometimes not. You must decide whether the amount of money in dispute justifies the loss of the employment.

Manufacturer's Representatives Who Sell to Mass Retailers

Approximately one mile from my office is the world headquarters for K-Mart Corporation[13]. I have handled several cases involving manufacturer's representatives who specialize in representing principals to K-Mart. These cases have involved toys, home products, home office supplies, and candy and related food products. In the mass merchandising business, just as in the automotive industry, it is important to understand the mechanics of how business is done.

In selling toys, for example, many of the purchasing decisions are made at Toy Fair in February of each year in New York. Additionally, there are selling fairs in the

---

[12] This is not necessarily true, as evidenced by Sharon Holland's continued employment at *Black Enterprise Magazine*. Continued employment without objection, however, can be a significant negative factor in the overall evaluation.

[13] At the time this book is being completed, K-Mart is in bankruptcy with major financial problems and an uncertain future.

Orient. The representative's role is to make a presentation along with the manufacturer and to attempt to convince the buyers to put the products of the manufacturer into a "planogram" or other purchasing system. Individual stores then order during the appropriate season. The big season for purchasing toys is September through December. Most of the selling by the manufacturer's representative takes place during the months of January through May. The orders are generally placed from May through September.

For candy, consumer products, home products, etc., the selling and buying systems are different, but the general system or procedure is usually the same. There is a several month period in which the selling by the manufacturer's representative is done and another several month period in which the purchasing is done by the individual stores.

The situation you want to avoid is to be in the position in which you have done the work during the selling season, but are terminated before the buying season and are not paid for the sales generated through your efforts.

Frequently in selling product to a company such as K-Mart or any of the other mass retailers, the most difficult part of the selling process is getting the principal's products into the retailer's system so that they can be ordered by the individual stores throughout the country. The manufacturer's representative's expertise is in having the contacts with the buyers and knowing what to do and when. Often success is the result of a concerted and organized effort by the manufacturer's representative to push the principal's product. Other times, success can be very opportunistic, resulting from the past relationship that the manufacturer's representative has with the buyers involved. I am personally aware of at least two instances in which the manufacturer's representative happened to be in the right place at the right time when a buyer was having a problem with another supplier. The representative was able to "solve the problem" by having his principal immediately begin shipping new product. This "opportunistic" result was only made possible because of the many years of hard work and effort which the manufacturer's representative had invested in calling on buyers at K-Mart on a regular and sometimes daily basis.

The goal of the manufacturer's representative is to get the product into the system so that large commissions can be earned for a long time. The goal of the manufacturer often seems to be to have the representative get the product into the system so that the manufacturer's direct personnel can handle the sales and then save the commission expense. Obviously, there is a significant conflict between these goals.

There are several ways a manufacturer's representative can protect himself when dealing with principals who sell to mass retailers. Some of these are as follows:

1. Be sure that your sales representation agreement has a minimum term of representation. For example, if the contract cannot be terminated for three or five years, and if you are successful

quickly, there would be a minimum term of compensation of three to five years.

2.   Limit the circumstances under which the agreement can be terminated. It's generally acceptable to be terminated for not being successful. You should not be terminated, however, for being successful unless adequate compensation is paid. Minimum performance criteria may be appropriate as long as the criteria are not unrealistically high nor beyond your control.

3.   Provide for the payment of post-termination commissions or compensation. At a minimum, this should include compensation for all orders received through any buying season for which you were the manufacturer's representative during the selling season. Further, at a minimum, you should also be sure to be appropriately paid for the period of time it took to get the principal established. For example, if you spent two years of effort to get the principal in the door, two years of post-termination commissions should be paid at a minimum.[14]

4.   If you cannot negotiate an acceptable contract, consider operating under an oral agreement stating that you will be paid for any sales generated through your efforts. This may provide sufficient flexibility allowing you to be paid a

---

[14] This presumes that no consulting fee or other front-end compensation is paid.

commission on the orders you were responsible for generating.

The key objective is to be fairly compensated for the benefits you have made possible for the principal to receive. The question to ask your principal is, "What is it worth to have your product sold by a major retailer?" You will almost always be in a better position to negotiate before you have performed rather than attempting to get paid after you have already accomplished your task. There is an inverse relationship between the value your principal places on your efforts before your task is accomplished compared to the value placed on your efforts after you have accomplished your task. Never defer your agreement on the commission rate until after your task has been completed.

You will find that some principals will not agree to any of the types of provisions discussed in this section. They have form contracts which provide for termination or thirty days notice with commissions being paid only for orders received as of the date of termination. These contracts should be avoided whenever possible.

Lawyers: To Involve, or Not to Involve?

Whether or not to engage a lawyer is obviously a significant issue for salespeople whenever they believe they have or will have a problem. Most salespeople are concerned about the cost of having a lawyer involved at the commencement stage of a relationship with either an employer or principal, as well as throughout the course of the relationship when problems exist.

It is not always necessary to hire a lawyer at the commencement of your relationship. This may depend upon whether you are the established and successful sales agency or the novice. Generally, the larger the dollars which are involved, the more important it is to obtain legal advice.

I would note that some of the best commission claims which I have handled have involved contracts or agreements which were not drafted by lawyers. It is not essential to have a lawyer draft your sales representative agreement, but if you can afford it, it is generally recommended.

Needless to say, once you are experiencing an acute problem regarding the failure to pay a commission or other significant problem with the relationship, it is important to obtain competent legal advice. There have been several situations in which I have been involved more than a year prior to a termination. In those circumstances, the sales representatives or manufacturer's representatives were astute enough to know that they would be having a problem down the road. We were able to position the claim over the following twelve months so as to put the client in the best possible position when the inevitable termination did occur.

There are no hard and fast answers as to when you should contact a lawyer. Generally you should trust your instinct. If you believe that you will be having a problem, then you probably will. Under these circumstances, I would highly recommend that you contact a competent legal professional at the earliest possible date.

2

Important Considerations in Written Sales Representation Agreements

If you are going to have a written sales representation agreement, there are several key considerations. The ones I believe are most important are explained below.

Exclusive Territory/Exclusive Accounts

Generally when I am negotiating a sales representation agreement for a manufacturer's representative, I try to make sure that the manufacturer's representative has either an exclusive territory or exclusive accounts. Usually this means that the salesperson would be entitled to a commission relative to any orders which are received from either the exclusive territory or the exclusive accounts without having to establish that the order was procured by the salesperson.

The problem is that, in many instances, there may be a combination of an outside and inside sales force. The outside sales force generally would be independent manufacturer's representatives. The inside sales force would ordinarily be the employee salespersons. An outside or independent manufacturer's representative is almost never in a position to effectively compete with an in-house salesperson at a specific account or in a specific territory. You should not be in a situation where you, as the independent representative, are calling on the same buyers or same accounts as the in-house salesperson unless you are getting paid a commission for all sales from the account or territory, regardless of whether the in-house salesperson was involved. Otherwise, the principal is in the position to direct the business to the in-house salesperson, ordinarily at less cost. This is generally a no-win situation for the manufacturer's representative.

I was involved in one case a few years ago in which a manufacturer's representative was representing a small family owned automotive supplier that manufactured injection molded plastic parts. My client took the owner's son on some sales calls to his automotive customers. The owner's son was the sales manager. My client introduced the owner's son to his customers and informed the customers that they could contact either the manufacturer's representative or the sales manager because they were working together as a team. One customer then sent a request for a quotation directly to the sales manager. The principal took the position that the resulting order was procured by the sales manager and not by the manufacturer's representative. We were successful in getting the manufacturer's representative his commissions, but the problem could have been avoided. The manufacturer's representative should have made sure there was a clear agreement, preferably in writing, that the manufacturer's representative was entitled to be paid a commission on all sales to his exclusive accounts.

The same principle can apply to territory agreements, although generally not to the same extent. If an independent sales representative agency is actively marketing its principal's products in a territory, it is often quite difficult to determine whether the order or account which is received or established is as a result of the independent salesperson's marketing and sales efforts or because of the efforts of the in-house salesperson. In order to avoid these problems, you should be sure that you get paid a commission for any business done in your territory.

I have one client who mails promotional material, sometimes including photographs and videotapes, to prospective customers. Such promotional activities can both directly and indirectly generate sales. You should be compensated for the indirect sales generated by your efforts as well as for the direct sales whenever possible.

Changes in Ownership of Customers

A change in the ownership of a customer can raise a significant issue as to the commission entitlement on shipments when the new owner is not on the sales representative's customer list. This can arise quite regularly in the automotive industry.

There has been a gradual consolidation of the automotive supply base in the last several years. There seems to have been a trend for the major OEMs to use fewer and necessarily larger suppliers. Some of these larger suppliers have merged with other suppliers; formed joint ventures or other strategic alliances; or have simply purchased smaller suppliers. In many cases the parts, tooling, plant locations and even buyers remain the same and only the name of the customer changes. In some instances there have been multiple ownership changes over the course of only a few years. This problem insofar as it relates to the change in the ownership of your principal is addressed later in this chapter in the section entitled "Successor Liability". In this section, I will address the change in ownership of one of your customer or account locations. This is an issue which should be addressed in your sales representation agreement.

A typical scenario may be helpful. Let's assume for example, that customer A is included in your exclusive list of customers and you have recently procured a large purchase order. Customer A is then purchased by customer B (in some cases because of the new business which you have recently secured) who is not on your exclusive list of customers. Do you get paid a commission on the sales which occur after the change in ownership? This may depend on whether your sales representation agreement addresses this circumstance.

In one of my cases from a few years ago, we dealt with this exact problem. This was in the case of Engineered Components & Lubricants v Consolidated Industrial Corporation. Our office filed this case in the Wayne

County Circuit Court in Detroit, Michigan. One of my client's exclusive accounts was Excel Automotive located in Pikeville, Tennessee. My client procured a large purchase order for window regulators from Excel Automotive for one of the vehicle programs. After the business had been secured, Excel was purchased by Dura Automotive Systems. Dura was not on my client's exclusive customer list. One of the issues was whether or not my client was entitled to a commission on the sales of the parts covered by the purchase order procured by my client when it was the Excel account notwithstanding the fact that the sales are now being made to the Dura account albeit at the same location.

The principal, Consolidated Industrial Corporation, tried to avoid commissions on two theories. The first theory was that since Dura was not on my client's customer list, no commissions were due. Secondly, they relied upon a provision in the sales representation agreement which allowed for the designation of accounts as "house accounts". This house account issue in this same case is addressed and discussed later in this chapter in the section entitled "Appropriation of House Accounts". In this particular case we were able to satisfactorily resolve the claim for my client. As a result of the issues dealt with in this case, we now include a provision in sales representation agreements for our clients to address changes in ownership of customers or accounts.

I have included some suggested language below to address this problem in a general fashion. This should be tailored by your lawyer to your specific circumstances and the particular industry involved. My suggested language is as follows:

> The change in the ownership of a customer or account shall not affect the payment of commissions due to the sales representative.

This should protect the commission entitlement on a commissionable part or program under the sales representation agreement. Careful attention should be paid to the specific language in the sales representation agreement regarding the prerequisites to commission entitlement. Any language you use should take into consideration the idiosyncrasies of your sales representation agreement.

You should be careful however, about using the change in ownership provision to seek a commission on parts or programs which were procured by other sales representatives or were procured directly by your principal. The language I suggested should be used as a "shield" to protect your commissions on parts or programs you have procured. I would not recommend that it be used as a "sword" to assert a claim for a commission on parts or programs you were not involved in. This could cause a significant and unnecessary conflict with your principal or other sales representative which could damage your relationship with your principal.

Call Reports

The degree to which principals require call reports varies significantly. Many manufacturer's representatives are reluctant to provide detailed information in call reports because they are fearful it can lay a foundation for the principal to handle the sales directly. I generally agree that this is a significant concern. Additionally, there are circumstances under which a manufacturer's representative's status as an independent contractor could be in jeopardy. If the IRS were to determine that the principal exerted too much control over the day-to-day operations and details of the manufacturer's representative's daily activities, then the manufacturer's representative could be deemed to be an employee rather than an independent contractor. This frankly is more of a problem for the principal than the manufacturer's representative.

Generally, a more important consideration is the need to protect the value of that which the manufacturer's representative brings to the table. This is usually the knowledge of the customer account and the prior experience of the manufacturer's representative. I have seen instances in which detailed call reports are used to gather as much information as possible about programs, key decision makers, customer needs, and other details of the efforts of the representative, so as to make it easier to terminate him and establish an in-house sales force. Ordinarily, you should be reluctant to provide any information which can be used to terminate you and replace you with an in-house sales force. There is no question that this can be a very sensitive area. The principal can have very legitimate reasons for seeking the information. Further, you do not want to appear to be too paranoid. The best advice I can give you regarding this issue is to be aware of the problem and to make the best decision under the circumstances.

Commission Rates: Percentage of Profit or Percentage of Sales?

In most cases salespeople are paid a percentage of the net sales price. In other instances they are paid a percentage of the margin or profit. In my opinion, it is generally better to be paid a commission based upon a percentage of the sales price rather than a percentage of the profit. The problem is that profit, markup, or margin can in some instances be very difficult to determine and is often under the complete control of the principal or manufacturer. One of the key considerations is the manner by which the profit, margin, or markup is determined. If "profit" is the selling price less cost of materials, it may not be a significant problem.

Once other factors are taken into consideration, such as overhead, cost of sales, and other intangible costs, it is virtually impossible to determine whether you are being properly compensated. For example, if costs can include general overhead and administrative expenses, the principal, especially in a small business, can significantly increase his salary and ultimately eliminate the profit upon which commission would be paid. I would normally recommend that you resist being paid a commission based upon the percentage of the profit, markup, or margin.

Commission Rates: Should Your Sales Representation Agreement Include a Commission Calculated on a Descending Scale?

It is common for many principals to seek to have a graduated commission scale included in the agreement with their manufacturer's representatives. Such a commission scale starts out at a higher rate on lower sales and gradually reduces to a smaller commission rate on higher volume sales. This is typically referred to as a graduated commission scale on a descending basis.

Frankly, I have always been somewhat perplexed by this concept. Recently I participated in a meeting between a client and the new owner of a principal. The principal wanted to meet with my client and me without his attorney present. He knew of me and respected my opinion. His original plan was to have a graduated commission scale on a descending basis.

First of all, I asked him what his principal objective was. He said that it was to motivate the salespeople to obtain as much new business as possible. I then asked him if that was the case, why he would want to provide a disincentive for his salespeople to go out and obtain large amounts of new business. The harder they work, the lower their commission rate would be. I advised him that if his real intention was to motivate his salespeople to obtain large amounts of new business, that the commission rate should be graduated on an *ascending* basis. This means that the more business which was obtained, the higher the commission rate would be. If he really wanted to motivate his salespeople, this would be the way to do it. The principal agreed with my analysis and decided to rethink his commission plan.

You will find that many salespeople who operate under agreements with commissions calculated on a descending scale will attempt to obtain a sufficient diversity of business from the various principals they represent in order to maintain commissions at the highest percentage rate for each principal. Frankly, I am not sure whether or not their principals recognize this is happening. The principals are probably wondering why sales and commissions have plateaued.

In my opinion, descending scale commission structures often are the result of the principal's objectives being somewhat skewed. Often the principal seems to be more concerned with the amount of commissions being paid to the manufacturer's representative rather than with the total amount of the sales and overall profitability. Any manufacturer's representative who makes more money than the sales manager he reports to knows that this can sometimes create great difficulty. In other cases, the reason for the descending scale commission plan is that the principal will grant price breaks to its customers on large volume orders. It often seems, however, that there is little or no correlation between the price break and the commission reduction.

If the principal is truly interested in maximizing sales, the best way to motivate its sales representatives to obtain larger sales volumes is to increase the commission rate on larger volume business. Presumably with larger volumes the relative costs of the principal should be decreased and there should be more room in the margin for an increased commission. I very seldom, however, see this occurring. It is almost always the opposite.

Most principals will find that they seem to need more manufacturer's representatives if they use a descending scale commission plan. The incentive for the manufacturer's representative is to increase his principal base to try to have as many principals as possible paying commissions at the higher commission rate, i.e., less volume of sales per principal. This is often a great benefit for the manufacturer's representative, because while he is attempting to maximize his commission rates, he is also diversifying his principal base. This makes his business less vulnerable to fluctuations in sales for an individual principal or industry. The net effect of this system for the principal, however, is to generally increase the overall commission expense. This is because the principal will be paying more manufacturer's representatives at higher rates for smaller sales volumes. Accordingly, a system which the principal normally believes will reduce overall commission expense as sales increase will often have the opposite effect.

The next time you are faced with a situation where your principal is attempting to negotiate a graduated commission scale with a lower commission rate being applied as sales increase, you should probably have a heart-to-heart discussion with your principal. If his purpose is to demotivate you, then he will likely be successful. Too many times I have seen situations where the principal is seeking to have the manufacturer's representative significantly increase sales but at the same time is decreasing the commission rate. In the event that you do have the opportunity to discuss this issue with your principal and he happens to turn a deaf ear to your discussion of the demotivating nature of the reduced commission rate on higher volume sales, I would not suggest that you push this. I would suggest that you let him continue to ponder in the future why sales seem to have plateaued.

Choice of Law and Where Action Is to Be Commenced

Many sales representation agreements have provisions which mandate that the law of the principal's state will be used and that any litigation must be commenced in the state where the principal is located. These types of provisions should be resisted if at all possible. It is generally better to sue in your home town than in another state. Further, the laws can vary from jurisdiction to jurisdiction. For example, many other states do not follow the Michigan Procuring Cause Doctrine. Generally, Michigan law historically has been relatively favorable for sales representatives and other manufacturer's representatives. Many other state laws are not. All other things being equal, you should try to litigate in your home town if possible.

Arbitration Clauses

Many sales representation agreements contain mandatory arbitration clauses. In general, my view of arbitration provisions in sales representation agreements is that I am opposed to them if they require arbitration through one of the national arbitration associations. There are three key reasons for this.

1. There is a relatively high nonrefundable filing fee. In some cases the fee can be more than $10,000. The filing fee for a court case is approximately $200. In addition, there are generally processing fees and other administrative fees as well as the costs of the arbitrators. In some cases, it can be more expensive for the manufacturer's sales representative to arbitrate a claim than to litigate it. This is because you generally pay an hourly fee for the arbitrators, but not for a judge or jury. Arbitrators' fees can be $200 to $300 or more per hour per arbitrator.

2. Unless specifically provided for in the sales representative agreement, the claimants and their counsel may have little control over the selection of the arbitrators. Ordinarily selection of the arbitrators is made from a list supplied by the arbitration association. The parties or their attorneys can generally strike those who are not acceptable and prioritize the acceptable ones. I would rather select an arbitrator irrespective of any list supplied by an arbitration association.

3.   I personally believe that there is an inherent institutional bias in favor of large employer/principal organizations and against the individual salesperson. It is important for me to state here that this is my own personal opinion and I have no objective facts upon which it is based. This makes logical sense, however, when you consider that the key markets for the national arbitration associations are larger employers and/or larger manufacturing organizations /principals. It is to the arbitration association's advantage to have a mandatory arbitration clause in all of the contracts which the larger employer/principal-oriented organizations have with their sales representatives. The best way for the national arbitration associations to continue to receive this type of business is for the arbitration panels to rule in a fashion which is relatively more favorable to the employer/principal than to the sales representative when compared to the result likely to be obtained in a trial in front of a judge or jury. Conversely, if the arbitration panels generally ruled in favor of the sales representative comparatively speaking, then there would be a disincentive for the employer/principal to use the arbitration association.

It is important to note that I am not suggesting that there is a conspiracy of any kind against sales representatives in the national arbitration associations. Most of the arbitrators are decent, honorable people who genuinely try to do what is right and fair based upon the evidence and all of the circumstances. Additionally, the case managers are generally very courteous and cooperative. I personally prefer, however, to avoid arbitrating through the national associations whenever possible. You cannot ignore the economic incentive on the part of the arbitration association for the ultimate result to be in favor of the principal/employer.

Even though I am generally opposed to arbitrating through the national associations, I am not opposed to arbitration in general. Often arbitration can be a relatively inexpensive, efficient, and effective way to resolve a business conflict such as a sales commission dispute. If I have control over the language to be used in the arbitration agreement, I prefer to have a three-member panel. With a three-member panel, one arbitrator should be selected by the sales representative, one arbitrator selected by the principal, and the neutral arbitrator selected by the two arbitrators designated by the parties. It is generally understood that the arbitrator selected by the sales representative will be an advocate for the sales representative and the arbitrator selected by the principal will be an advocate for the principal. Under these circumstances, the job of the sales representative's arbitrator, as well as of the principal's arbitrator, is to convince the neutral arbitrator of the merits of their respective sides. I generally prefer to have a retired judge act as the neutral arbitrator. A retired judge gives the panel more credibility.

Some readers may think that lawyers in general may be opposed to arbitration because it gives the lawyers less opportunity to engage in expensive discovery[15] and therefore to build up their fee. In my practice, however, this could not be farther from the truth. Virtually all of my commission cases are handled on a contingent fee basis. This means that the more "busy work" which is done, the lower my effective hourly rate becomes. My incentive is to obtain the best possible recovery for my client in the least possible time. It is counterproductive to my clients' interests, and therefore to my interests, to unnecessarily delay a final resolution or to make the process more costly than necessary.

For the larger commission disputes, i.e., those involving claims of $250,000 or more, it is especially important to be able to obtain the necessary discovery before the arbitration hearing. Lawyers do not like surprises. Discovery is readily obtainable if the claim is litigated through the court system, but it may be difficult to obtain if the matter is arbitrated. In large cases, I generally prefer that the sales representation agreement contain no mandatory arbitration provision. This allows me to obtain the necessary discovery during the course of a lawsuit. If after discovery is completed, the parties desire to have their dispute resolved by an arbitration panel as opposed to a judge or a jury, the appropriate arbitration agreement can be entered into at that time.

---

15 "Discovery" is a legal term for the process by which opposing sides in litigation obtain and exchange information concerning the dispute. In my cases, discovery primarily consists of obtaining the sales information necessary to calculate the commissions due.

Jack Ciupak & Associates v. First Inertia Switch Limited

There are certain circumstances in which it may be more advisable to arbitrate a claim rather than to litigate it in court. One such example was a case I handled entitled *Jack Ciupak & Associates v First Inertia Switch Limited.* In the *Jack Ciupak* case we filed an action in the Wayne County Circuit Court in Michigan, which is generally a very favorable venue for plaintiffs. In this case, however, we had a rather unusual circumstance. Jack Ciupak & Associates was a small manufacturer's representative agency owned by Jack Ciupak and his wife Bess. Ciupak had an agreement with First Inertia Switch to act as its exclusive manufacturer's representative for the sale of fuel cut-off switches and other sensors to automotive customers and in particular to Ford Motor Company, located in Wayne County. First Inertia Switch Limited (FISL) sold fuel cut-off switches used to prevent vehicle fires. FISL was owned by a holding company located in the United Kingdom. One of the other companies they owned was First Technology Safety Systems (FTSS). FTSS manufactured anthropomorphic test devices commonly referred to as "crash-test dummies." At one time Ciupak represented both FISL and FTSS.

After FTSS canceled its agreement with Ciupak and paid the post-termination commissions, Ciupak lent the sum of $100,000 from his profit-sharing trust to a competitor of FTSS. The competitor was formed by some of Ciupak's friends, who had previously worked at FTSS. Eventually, FTSS sued the competitor and during the course of discovery found out about the loan Ciupak made through his profit-sharing trust to the competitor. Once the holding company found out about Ciupak's loan, they terminated the contract between FISL and Ciupak. FISL contended that Ciupak breached the contract and that the termination was "for cause" based upon the loan by Ciupak's profit-sharing trust to the competitor of FTSS. The case against FISL proceeded to mandatory mediation, which at that time in the State of Michigan meant that three attorneys evaluated the case for settlement purposes. There was a relatively small mediation award of approximately $160,000. This was totally unacceptable because the termination commissions under Ciupak's contract with FISL were approximately $1,000,000. We obviously rejected the mediation award and were planning to proceed to trial.

In this case we agreed to arbitrate the claim because I knew that FISL was going to assert that Ciupak committed a major act of disloyalty by making the loan to the competitor of FTSS, the affiliated company. Under Ciupak's contract, however, there was no basis to avoid the payment of the commissions based upon the loan to the competitor of FTSS. FISL and FTSS, although owned by the same holding company, were two separate and legally distinct entities. I was very concerned, however, about the ability of a jury to separate the issues and felt that a jury might agree that Ciupak acted disloyally and might decide for FISL in our claim for commissions. I agreed to arbitrate the claim in front of a panel of two lawyers and one retired Wayne County Circuit Court judge. I selected one of the attorney arbitrators and FISL selected the other and both attorneys agreed upon the retired Wayne County Circuit judge as the neutral arbitrator.

This is a totally acceptable procedure and these arbitrators are known as party-appointed arbitrators and are expected to be inclined to favor the party who appointed them. This is consistent with Rule R-12 of the Commercial Arbitration Rules of the American Arbitration Association. My principal objective was to convince the judge of the merits of our claim because we generally expected that the arbitrators appointed by both parties would be somewhat of an advocate for the side which appointed them. I felt much more comfortable having the judge decide the case rather than a jury because the loan was not a violation of Ciupak's legal obligations under the agreement. I was confident that the judge would disregard the emotional "disloyalty" argument and make the decision based strictly upon the language of the contract. I was not confident at all that a jury would be able to do this. The strategy was successful, and we received an arbitration award of approximately $965,000. Additionally, after we got into the case we were able to determine that some pre-termination commissions were not properly paid. We filed a subsequent lawsuit which we were able to resolve. I cannot disclose the resolution of the second lawsuit due to the fact that we agreed to a confidentiality clause in the resolution agreement.

In Ciupak's case, we obtained a substantially better result in arbitration than I believe we would have been able to obtain in front of a jury. This is an example of a circumstance in which a sales representative was better off arbitrating his claim rather than having a jury trial. You should discuss this issue thoroughly with your lawyer before making any decision as to whether to arbitrate a claim rather than to litigate it. In this case, FISL, I believe, was interested in an arbitration because the process is somewhat more streamlined and it eliminated the volatility of a jury. Apparently FISL believed that they would have a better chance in front of the arbitration panel. I clearly felt that our side had a much better chance in an arbitration than we would have had in front of a jury.

As noted earlier, if I am going to arbitrate a claim I generally prefer to have the parties each select one of the arbitrators and then the two arbitrators select a neutral arbitrator, preferably a retired Circuit Court judge. My criteria for the plaintiff's arbitrator are as follows:

- I want the arbitrator I select to know me personally;

- The arbitrator I select should be a successful litigation attorney who has handled large cases, e.g., claims involving one million dollars or more, on a regular basis, preferably for a contingent fee; and

- I want the arbitrator to be a well-respected attorney with an impeccable reputation so that he will have credibility with the chairperson of the arbitration panel.

My criteria for the neutral arbitrator or chairperson are as follows:

- I prefer the neutral to be a retired trial judge. As stated earlier, this gives the arbitration panel more credibility to the clients;

- I want the chairperson to have an impeccable reputation for integrity, decisiveness and even handedness; and

- Ideally, I would like the chairperson to have had experience with me professionally. This just means that I would prefer to have appeared before the judge in other cases, so that he knows me professionally.

The reason why I want the neutral arbitrator or chairperson to have had prior experience with me professionally is that generally my credibility has already been established. I want the judge to know that sales commission disputes are virtually the only cases which I handle and that I am considered to be an expert in commission disputes. Most importantly, if I indicate that I can prove a fact, I want the judge to have some history with me so that he will know what I say can be believed.

Successor Liability

An increasingly important consideration in any manufacturer's representative or other sales representation agreement, is the liability for commission payments in the event that the assets of the manufacturer or principal are sold. During a recent twelve-month period, I had five pending cases involving successor liability issues.

The problem generally arises regarding manufacturer's representatives. My experience usually has been in the circumstances in which the manufacturer's representative has been very successful in obtaining new business. Primarily, this has been in the automotive industry. Future sales potential for an automotive supplier who has been awarded a purchase order for a production part can be substantial over the life of part.

Often with the acquisition of the new business, the financial outlook for a small automotive parts supplier can increase substantially. This can give the owners the opportunity to attempt to market the business based upon the new programs which have been awarded and the projected future sales revenue and profit.

If an established supplier can purchase the business of the principal and blend it into its existing facilities and capacity using its existing sales force, there can be substantial savings. A significant factor can be the reduced sales commission expense. The intent of the buyer generally is to have its sales force handle the business at little or no additional expense. The commission savings then go directly to the bottom line of the purchasing company. Unfortunately, this necessarily means that the manufacturer's representative who procured the business will be terminated. It is important that the sales representation agreement contain adequate language to protect the manufacturer's representative's commission in the event of such a sale or transfer of the business or assets. This is one circumstance in which it is best to have a well-worded successor liability clause in the contract in order to protect your recovery of commissions.[16]

If there is merely a sale of stock of the principal corporation, this should not have a major impact upon your sales representation agreement. As long as your agreement was with the corporation, the fact that the ownership of the corporation changes should have no significant effect.

Most of these types of transactions, however, involve a sale of assets. There is generally a purchase agreement specifically identifying the assets to be purchased and the liabilities to be assumed. Normally, the assets purchased include the equipment and contracts of the principal, but often exclude the liability to the sales representative. Ordinarily, courts will attempt to enforce the intent of the parties to the purchase or sale agreement. If the manufacturer's representative agreement does not have a sufficient successor liability clause, even though you may

---

[16] This is one key disadvantage of an oral sales representation agreement or letter agreement. See Chapter One.

have a "life of part" contract with your principal, there may be no basis for a commission claim after the sale of assets. This is because the principal is no longer manufacturing the parts. Most sales representation agreements provide that commissions are calculated on the net sales. If the principal is no longer manufacturing a product and making sales, no commissions ordinarily would be due.

To address this problem in the manufacturer's representative agreements I prepare, I generally include language regarding successor liability. An example is as follows:

> This agreement shall be binding upon the parties hereto as well as their respective successors, assigns, asset purchasers and joint venturers. Specifically, in the event of the sale, transfer or conveyance of any of the assets or business of the principal commissionable to the representative, this agreement shall be binding upon the purchaser, successor, transferee, asset purchaser or joint venture to the same extent as it would be binding upon the principal if no sale, transfer or conveyance of the assets or business had taken place. It is the intent of the parties hereto that the representative's right to termination commissions be specifically protected in the event of any such sale, transfer, conveyance, asset purchase or joint venture and that the commissions shall be paid in full by the purchaser, successor, transferee, asset purchaser or joint venture. The principal shall timely notify any purchaser, successor, transferee or joint venture of the obligations

pursuant to this agreement. In the event that
the purchaser, successor, transferee or joint
venture does not pay the post-termination
commissions, then the post-termination
commissions shall be paid by the principal.

It is important to note here that this language has not
been tested in any court. My client however, clearly has
a better chance of protecting his commissions if the above
language is used then he does if the sales representation
agreement does not address this issue.

You will often find some reluctance by your principal to
agree to language of this sort. The practical effect of
successor liability language is that it makes it more
difficult for the principal to market the business. The
important consideration from your standpoint as the
salesperson, however, is that the sale of the business
should have no impact upon whether you get paid the
post-termination commissions provided for in your sales
representation agreement.

One recent case which my office handled should be
mentioned here. This is the case of *Zimmermann & Sons v
Diversified Decorative Plastics*, which was pending in the
Federal District Court for the Eastern District of
Michigan, Southern Division, in Detroit.

Zimmermann & Sons was a sales agency owned by two
cousins, Ralph Zimmermann and Rob Zimmermann,
whose fathers started the business. The sales agency had
a decent contract with Shawnee Plastics in Kentucky, but
Shawnee was always behind in commissions due to
financial problems.

Shawnee Plastics entered into an agreement to sell its assets to a new company formed for the specific purpose of buying the assets and continuing the business. The new company, Diversified Decorative Plastics, purchased all of the plant and equipment including the purchase orders with the automotive customers. They did not, however, purchase any liabilities. This means that the new company did not agree to pay existing or future sales commissions to Zimmerman & Sons.

The new owners had no existing sales force, however, and initially kept Zimmermann & Sons as the sales representatives after the closing. One of the principal reasons for this is that the new owners did not know the buyers for the automotive customers. Additionally, it was evident that the customers had legitimate concerns about the ability of the new owners to perform under the existing purchase orders. The only real connection the customers had was with the sales representatives.

Zimmermann & Sons were asked to introduce the new owners and managers to the customers and to help to get all of the purchase orders transferred from Shawnee Plastics to the new entity. Shortly after the Zimmermanns were able to accomplish the transfer of the purchase orders, they were terminated when they were unable to reach a new sales representation agreement with the new owners.

We filed suit against the new owners seeking continuing commissions on the business which the Zimmermanns had obtained for Shawnee Plastics and which had been transferred to the new owners. Because of the fact that the Zimmermanns were kept on during the transition period, we were able to take the position that the Zimmermanns had procured the purchase orders for the new owners by convincing the customers to transfer the purchase orders from Shawnee to the new entity. We were in a substantially stronger position then we would have been if Zimmermanns would have been terminated immediately after the acquisition. In my opinion, the new owners wanted to accept the benefits of the Zimmermanns' efforts, but without the obligation to compensate them on the continuing sales at a level acceptable to the Zimmermanns. We ultimately were able to work out an acceptable resolution for our client.

It is extremely important to obtain competent legal advice whenever it appears as though the assets or business of your principal or employer will be sold. Fortunately for the Zimmermanns, they had contacted me well over a year in advance of the transaction. We were able to keep them properly positioned to obtain the best possible result under the circumstances when the termination did in fact occur.

Obtaining a Security Interest in the Orders You Procure

Another problem which has been significant lately for some of my clients has been the bankruptcy of their principal. Two major bankruptcies of automotive suppliers in southeastern Michigan have involved Cambridge Industries and Key Plastics. These occurred, at least partially, as a result of a recent drop in automotive sales. The typical problem arises when a manufacturer's representative is responsible for procuring a substantial amount of new business, and this can be in the tens of millions of dollars in sales. In some cases, automotive suppliers can grow too big, which means that there may be cash flow problems or other financial problems generally due to insufficient capitalization.

If the supplier goes into bankruptcy, ordinarily the claim of the manufacturer's representative for commissions on continuing business is in substantial jeopardy. Many companies will purchase the assets of a bankrupt manufacturer or automotive supplier through the bankruptcy system in order to purge the pre-existing liabilities. Many of the liabilities which are sought to be purged include the continuing commission obligations to the manufacturer's representative.

Working with bankruptcy counsel, I have come up with a provision which I am attempting to have put into as many manufacturer's representative agreements as possible. It is a relatively simple provision which grants to the manufacturer's representative a security interest in the proceeds of any sales generated as a result of purchase orders procured by my clients. This puts the representative in the position of a secured creditor, which gives some additional protection in the event of the bankruptcy of the principal. The language I am currently using, but which has not yet been tested in court, is set forth below. Again, there is no guarantee that this language will work, but it will at least put the manufacturer's representative in a better position than if

no security agreement were entered into. The language
is as follows:

> **Security Interest.** Manufacturer grants to Sales
> Representative a security interest in the
> proceeds of the sale of any products which it
> manufactures, sells or distributes as a result of
> orders received from Sales Representative's
> exclusive accounts listed on Exhibit A. The
> purpose of this provision is to secure the
> payment of commissions to Sales
> Representative pursuant to this Agreement.
> Manufacturer agrees to execute a UCC-
> Financing Statement as well as any other
> documentation which is reasonably necessary
> in order to perfect the security interest herein
> granted.

Many principals will be reluctant to agree to this type of
language. In fact, in some instances it may constitute a
violation of the principal's lending agreements to grant
additional security in their assets. You may be required
to subordinate your security interest to that of your
principal's bank. My philosophy, however, is, "Nothing
ventured, nothing gained." There may be circumstances
in which you may want to have your lawyer put this type
of provision into your agreement. It is very important to
be sure that you perfect the security interest in
accordance with the laws of your state. This generally
means recording the security interest with the Secretary
of State or Register of Deeds office.

Non-competition Agreements/Covenants Not to Compete

Many sales representation agreements and many employment agreements contain provisions limiting the ability of the manufacturer's representative or employee, to compete with his or her principal /employer. There are two time periods which typically are applicable. These are prohibitions against competition during the term of the agreement and prohibitions against competition after termination.

Even in the event that the sales representation agreement or employment agreement does not specifically prohibit competition during the term of the agreement, the representation of a competing principal or employer would generally be prohibited by implication, at the very least. Obviously, an employee cannot work for two employers, especially competing ones, at the same time. Similarly, a manufacturer's representative should never be in a position in which he is representing competing principals while calling on a buyer. This is addressed in more detail in Chapter Four, in the section entitled **Eliminating Conflict of Interest Issues.**

As a general rule, non-competition agreements and covenants not to compete are enforceable. In Michigan, for many years, there was a statute which prohibited such agreements as a matter of public policy. The only exception was agreements not to compete which were incidental to the sale of a business. The statute has been repealed and now such agreements are legal as long as they are reasonable and reasonably related to a legitimate employer interest. You must assume that any such agreement you sign is enforceable, although there are defenses which can be asserted under certain circumstances. We have been successful in opposing these on occasion, but as a general rule agreements not to compete are enforceable.

If I am negotiating an agreement for a manufacturer's representative, I generally try to limit the non-competition to business already awarded. This means that the manufacturer's representative would not be able to try to move the existing business from the old principal to the new principal. He would, however, be able to complete on new business. The manufacturer's representative will need to replace the income lost as a result of the termination. In the automotive industry there is generally at least a two- to three-year lead time on obtaining any significant new business. If you are out of the industry for an extended period of time, you may lose your contacts. It is generally not advisable to agree not to compete on new business after termination.

For an employee, there should be additional consideration or compensation covering the non-competition period subsequent to termination. For example, if you are prohibited from competing for one year, there should be the continuation of your salary or commissions during the one-year period. You should try to avoid agreeing to a provision which effectively prohibits you from engaging in the only business with which you are familiar. Under these circumstances, you can become a virtual indentured employee with no ability to improve your employment situation.

When it comes to non-competition agreements, this is one circumstance in which you should have an experienced lawyer review your agreement before you sign it.

Appropriation of House Accounts

There is no point in having a good termination payout provision if your principal can appropriate your accounts or your territory without compensation. Ultimately what could occur is that all of your accounts or territory could be appropriated and there would not be any remaining business upon which you would be paid a commission during your "life of part" commission arrangement. Generally, your agreement should provide that territory adjustments or the appropriation of house accounts can only be done by mutual agreement. Further, the appropriation of the house account or territory should trigger the termination provision in your agreement. This means that if you are to receive commissions for any specific period of time after termination, the appropriation of a house account is considered to be a termination as to that account. The post-termination commission payout should be applicable to those account appropriation circumstances.

A recent case our office handled is a good example of a problem which can arise from liberal language allowing the principal to unilaterally designate accounts as house accounts. This is the case of *Engineered Components & Lubricants v. Consolidated Industrial Corporation*, which was

filed in the Wayne County Circuit Court in Detroit,
Michigan.

The key issue in this case dealt with whether the
principal had the unlimited right to designate an account
as a house account at any time and to eliminate the
payment of all commissions to the manufacturer's
representative. The key contractual language was as
follows:

> St. Clair [St. Clair Plastics was a division of
> Consolidated Industrial Corporation] reserves
> the right to negotiate and sell direct to Fisher
> Body Division of General Motors Corporation
> or any customer now or hereafter designated as
> a "house account", which designation may be
> applied by St. Clair to individual orders or
> sales made direct by St. Clair. No commissions
> shall be due or payable on shipments made to,
> or orders received from, a "house account."

The principal eliminated all commissions on the Excel
account in Tennessee after Excel was purchased by Dura
Automotive Systems. The principal contended that it
could designate any account as a house account at any
time and eliminate immediately thereafter the payment
of all commissions. Our position was that such a house
account designation could be made prospectively but not
retroactively. This means that any new business which
the principal obtained "direct", i.e., not through the
efforts of the manufacturer's representative prior to the
designation of the account as a house account, would not
be commissionable. Existing business obtained through
the efforts of the manufacturer's representative was to be

paid for "life of part" subject to the termination provision in the contract.

Commissions of approximately $65,000 were at issue, together with the $100,000 in additional damages under the Michigan Sales Representative Commission Act for an intentional failure to pay past due commissions after termination, together with costs and attorney fees. Fortunately for the manufacturer's representative, there was some history regarding the prior designation of a house account by the principal. In the prior instance, the sales manager for the principal agreed in writing that the manufacturer's representative would be paid a commission for "life of part" on all existing business obtained by the representative prior to the designation of the account as a house account. Commissions were then eliminated on any new business obtained by the principal "direct" after the designation of the account as a house account.

We ultimately settled the case and netted to my client substantially more than his unpaid commissions. The result could have been different if not for the prior history of continuing commissions on the business procured by the manufacturer's representative prior to the designation of an account as a house account.

This is an important lesson for manufacturer's representatives. You cannot agree to language in your sales representation agreement which allows the principal to avoid the post-termination commission payout provision of your contract by including a provision which liberally allows the principal to designate accounts as house accounts. Such a house account designation or appropriation must be treated as a termination, with the post-termination provisions of the agreement being applied. For example, if the post-termination provision of the agreement required the principal to pay commissions for three years after termination, the principal should be required to pay commissions for three years after appropriation of the account as a house account.

Termination: The Most Important Part of Your Contract

The typical language I generally prefer to include in my version of a sales representation agreement is set forth below. This is drafted with the idea that the sales representative is being paid "life of part" commissions:

> In the event of the termination of this agreement, representative shall be entitled to a commission for "life of part" for all parts, products, projects or programs which are in production as of the effective date of termination. The representative shall also be entitled to "life of part" commissions for all parts, products, projects, or programs for which an inquiry or request for a quotation was received prior to the effective termination date regardless of when production is commenced. Additionally, the representative shall be entitled to "life of part" commissions for any parts, products, projects or programs which representative can demonstrate it was actively working on as of the date of the receipt of the

> termination notice. Representative shall provide a list of such parts, products, projects or programs within 30 days after receiot of the termination notice.

The purpose for including the above language regarding requests for quotations or inquiries is to protect against a situation in which the manufacturer's representative is responsible for generating an inquiry which ultimately results in an order. For example, the inquiry may be for a new program for five to ten million dollars in annual sales. Once the principal is aware of the inquiry, it could terminate the representative and quote the job directly without including a commission, bypassing the representative. If the manufacturer's representative was responsible for generating the inquiry, he should be paid a commission regardless of whether he happens to be terminated prior to the time the job is quoted or the purchase order issued.

In many cases, the manufacturer's representative will work for years at the engineering stage trying to get his principal's products specified into a program. The inquiry or request for a quotation may not be issued until after the principal's products have already been specified. It is not fair to have the principal accept, without compensation, the benefits of the manufacturer's representative's efforts in obtaining the request for quotation.

If a lesser term than "life of part" is to be included in the agreement, the following could be used:

In the event of the termination of this agreement, the representative shall be entitled to post-termination commissions as follows:

(a) For all parts, products, projects or programs which are in production as of the effective date of termination, the principal shall pay to the representative a commission on all shipments made within 36 months from and after the effective date of termination regardless of when payment is made;

(b) For all parts, products, projects or programs for which an inquiry or request for a quotation was received prior to the effective termination date, the principal shall pay to the representative a commission on all shipments made within 36 months from and after the start of regular production, regardless of when payment is made.

(c) For all parts, products, projects or programs which representative was actually working on prior to receipt of the termination notice, the principal shall pay to the representative a commission on all shipments made within 36 months from and after the start of regular production, regardless of when payment is made. Representative shall provide a list of such parts, products, projects, or programs to the principal within 30 days of the receipt of the termination notice.

There is no point in having an agreement that gives you a fair commission rate if the principal can terminate the agreement at any time and be absolved of any liability to pay you commissions on business which you obtained. Too many times I have seen written sales representation agreements which allow a principal to terminate the agreement on thirty days notice without any further liability to the salesperson. As far as I am concerned, this is the worst possible event which can happen to a salesperson, whether an independent manufacturer's representative or an employee salesperson. There is nothing worse than spending years pursuing business only to be terminated without the payment of the commissions you were expecting, once the business is obtained. In fact, the principal focus of my practice is to prevent this from happening to my clients.

The key principle is that you should be paid for what you do. If it takes you three years to obtain a purchase order which will be generating sales for five years, your contract should be set up to require the principal to compensate you for at least a significant portion of that five-year period.

In many industries, there are no blanket purchase orders which will generate sales over a multiple month or multiple year time period. In those instances, each individual purchase order is an individual sale without any residual sales activity. Under these circumstances, your goal should be to make sure that any purchase orders you are responsible for generating prior to your effective termination date are commissionable. This should be irrespective of when the purchase orders are ultimately shipped and payment received. Michigan law is supportive of this position. In 1958, the Michigan Supreme Court issued its decision in *Reed vs. Kurdziel*, 89

N.W.2d 479 (Mich. 1958). This was a landmark decision addressing the Procuring Cause Doctrine as it relates to manufacturer's representatives and other salespersons. As indicated by Justice Cavanagh,

> The relationship between agent or broker and principal being a contractual one, it is immediately apparent that whether an agent or broker employed to sell personalty on commission is entitled to commissions on sales made or consummated by his principal or by another agent depends upon the intention of the parties and the interpretation of the contract of employment, and that, as in other cases involving interpretation, all the circumstances must be considered. * * * This rule is recognized and stated in the American Law Institute, 2 Restatement, Agency, §449, Comment a.

> It would appear that underlying all the decisions is the basic principle of fair dealing, preventing a principal from unfairly taking the benefit of the agent's or broker's services without compensation, and imposing upon the principal, regardless of the type of agency or contract, liability to the agent or broker for commissions for sales upon which the agent or broker was the procuring cause, notwithstanding the sales made have been consummated by the principal himself or some other agent. In Michigan, as well as in most jurisdictions, the agent is entitled to recover his commission whether or not he has personally concluded and completed the sale, it being sufficient if his efforts were the procuring cause

of the sale. *Reade v. Haak*, 147 Mich 42; *Case v. Rudolph Wurlitzer Co.*, 186 Mich 81; *MacMillan v. C. & G. Cooper Co.*, 249 Mich 594. In Michigan the rule goes further to provide if the authority of the agent has been canceled by the principal, the agent would nevertheless be permitted to recover the commission if the agent was the procuring cause. *Heaton v. Edwards*, 90 Mich 500; *McGovern v. Bennett*, 146 Mich 558; *MacMillan v. C. & G. Cooper Co., supra.*

Reed, supra, page 294, 295.

The Michigan courts have been generally supportive of protecting the entitlement of commissions for salespersons on sales which were procured by the salesperson for their principal/employer.

3

You Have an Agreement – Now What Do You Do?

Be Credible

It is important to keep in mind that you are always selling. You must sell yourself to your principal and you must sell your principal to your customers. In fact, it goes further than that. It is basic human nature to seek approval or affirmation of ourselves. Maybe this relates to some of our inherent insecurities, but it is part of what makes us human.

If we expect our point of view to be respected and to be listened to when we speak, then we must have credibility. Credibility or believability is an indispensable attribute for a good salesperson, or for an attorney, for that matter. After all, attorneys are salespeople also. My job is to sell my client and my client's case to a judge, jury, or arbitration panel. This is done by being prepared, by being honest, and by being trustworthy. If a judge, jury, or arbitration panel cannot trust what I say, then I cannot be an effective advocate for my client. Similarly, a manufacturer's representative or other salesperson will have difficulty in espousing the merits of a particular product if he does not gain the trust and respect of his customers.

Create a Good Record: The Story of the Three Umpires

I often relate to my clients the story of the three baseball umpires who were discussing how they call balls and strikes. The first umpire says, "I calls 'em as I sees 'em." The second umpire says, "I calls 'em as they are." The third umpire says, "They ain't nothin' till I calls 'em."

When it comes to establishing a claim for commissions, it does not always matter what happened. What matters most is what you can *prove* happened. You should always assume that you will have to justify in court at some point in time your claim for commissions. Create and maintain good records. You should always have copies of each purchase order you were responsible for obtaining. If possible, try to have your name included on the purchase order issued by the customer. Although this doesn't necessarily have any legal significance, it is persuasive in supporting your contention that you were responsible for obtaining a particular order.

When you receive a large purchase order from a customer, include a cover letter to your principal. For example:

Sample Letter

ABC Manufacturing Company
Anywhere, U.S.A.

Dear Principal:

Attached please find a purchase order which we recently obtained from A-1 Customer. Mr. Buyer told me that he is very impressed with our proposal and we should be the supplier of this product for as long as we do a good job. Our office has been able to position ABC Manufacturing Company so that we should receive new opportunities. We should be able to receive additional new business from our customer.

This particular part is expected to be in production for five years as long as we can maintain quality and delivery and are competitive in price.

We look forward to our future successes.

Very truly yours,

XYZ Sales Agency

It is also a good idea to write letters confirming key discussions with your principal. Any promises or commitments which have been orally made should be documented in writing. Remember Murphy's Law. Assume that you will be terminated and that you will have to fight to establish your claim for commissions. Contemporaneous correspondence, or even notes, can be very effective in establishing a claim. Do not allow your principal to be in a position in which he can rewrite history. You would be surprised by the number of instances that a principal or employer will attempt to establish that it was not the salesperson who obtained the purchase order, but the principal himself. A good record can help to counter this. Most lawsuits for commissions are won or lost long before the complaint is filed with the court.

Make Yourself Indispensable

One way to guard against termination is to make it very difficult for your principal or employer to be successful without you. You should be the one with the key relationships with your customers. You should do everything you can to make it very difficult to replace you. Try to have as much information come through you as possible. This may mean more work, but if you make it easy for your principal to deal directly with your customer, you will be more easily replaceable.

One of my clients is a young man who I will refer to as "Hector"[17]. In addition to his role as a manufacturer's representative in procuring new business, Hector got involved in many program management activities. Much of the work Hector performed was that which would ordinarily be performed by the principal. This included much of the day-to-day administration of the business he was responsible for procuring. All of the paperwork went through Hector's office and most of the contact with the customer was done by Hector. This was a substantial benefit when one of Hector's principals went into bankruptcy. The company that purchased the assets from his principal during the bankruptcy process needed Hector's assistance in transitioning the business to the new owner.

The problem for a manufacturer's representative under this scenario is that the bankruptcy process typically allows the purchaser of the principal's assets the option of rejecting the manufacturer's representative agreement as well as any other executory contracts.[18] This gives the asset purchaser the ability to retain the business but avoid future commission obligations. The position which Hector was able to put himself in by being an indispensable part of the relationship with the customer allowed him to receive a substantial payment to

---

[17] My client asked that his real name and the name of his principal not be used due to the fact that there are still some unresolved compensation issues.

[18] An executory contract is a contract which has not yet been fully performed.

transition the business to the new owner. This allowed him to recover a substantial part of his "commissions." If the program management work had been done by his principal, Hector would not have had the bargaining power to negotiate an acceptable transition agreement with the purchaser. This is an important lesson. If you are able to place yourself into a position in which your services are needed, you are in a much stronger bargaining position to be sure that you get paid in the event of any kind of a transition of ownership.[19]

Many manufacturer's representatives try to avoid additional responsibility and just want to sell. If you build a system around your services, then you may make it much more difficult for your principal or any purchaser to terminate your services in the event of an acquisition or other transfer of ownership.

Are You Sure You Are Being Paid the Proper Amount of Commission?

This may sound incredible, but some manufacturer's representatives have no idea whether they are being paid the proper amount of commissions by their principal. I was personally involved in at least three situations recently in which my client was receiving substantial commissions, sometimes at the rate of $60,000 to $70,000

---

[19] Due to the bankruptcy proceedings, the new owner was able to effectively eliminate the normal post-termination commissions for life of part which Hector would have received had he been terminated by the principal without filing for bankruptcy.

per month, and they did not know whether the checks were in the correct amount. Mediators, arbitrators, and judges who are involved in these cases have a tendency to react with disbelief when they are told that in some instances the representatives have no real idea as to whether they are being paid the proper amount of commissions in any given month. The unfortunate reality is that it happens probably more than many manufacturer's representatives are willing to admit.

The typical response by the manufacturer's representative when this type of problem is discovered generally falls into one of three categories:

- I trusted my principal to properly calculate my commissions.

- I do not have the time or staff to audit every commission payment.

- I did not want to antagonize my principal by questioning the amount of the payment.

The problem which is created when the manufacturer's representative does not verify his commission payments is that it can become very difficult to contest the payments at a later date.

In many instances, the fact that the commissions are not being properly paid does not necessarily mean that the principal is knowingly underpaying the representative's commissions. In some cases, there may be legitimate differences of opinion as to whether certain items may be commissionable or whether some costs may be deductible from the sales price. Often in the automotive industry, the automotive manufacturer who is dealing with a Tier One supplier[20] will prepare a monthly remittance advice and include this with the monthly payment to the supplier. Typically included with that remittance advice is an adjustment register with charges to the supplier. These may include charges for returns for credit, pricing adjustments, expenses to rework parts, premium freight expense, and other items. Some suppliers may take the adjustment register and subtract the adjustments from what otherwise would be the net sales price and then pay a commission on the adjusted balance. The problem is that some of the adjustments which are taken by the automotive customer may be properly credited against the sales price before calculating the commission, and others may not.

For example, typically pricing adjustments and returns for credit are properly subtracted from the gross sales amount before calculating the commissionable net sales. Other expenses which are charged back may not be properly deductible from the gross sales for commission calculation purposes, such as reworking expenses and premium freight expenses. The reworking expenses may be charges incurred by the automotive customer for sorting parts or conforming the parts to specification and should be the responsibility of the principal. Premium freight expense may be charged back to the supplier when the supplier is unable to meet production

---

[20] A Tier One supplier sells directly to an automotive OEM such as G.M., Ford, or DaimlerChrysler. A Tier Two supplier sells directly to a Tier One.

requirements on time. These expenses are not necessarily chargeable against the gross sales price for commission calculation purposes. The manufacturer's representative should not generally have his commissions affected when the principal is unable to meet quality or delivery requirements. More importantly, many sales representative agreements do not allow for these adjustments.

Many manufacturer's representatives do not sufficiently review adjustments which are taken against the gross sales price to determine whether all of the adjustments are properly deductible for commission calculation purposes.

Sufficient Backup Documentation

Any time you receive a commission payment from your principal, there should be sufficient documentation attached to the commission check which allows you to verify the amount of the commission payment. This does not necessarily require the inclusion of all invoices, but an invoice register should be included. My experience is that the invoice registers are generally accurate. Additionally, there should be an explanation for any adjustments to the invoice amount with supporting documentation.

Obviously, it would be most advisable to audit the commission payment on a monthly basis to verify that each month's commission payment has been accurately made. Many representatives, however, do not have sufficient staff to do this. This is where Murphy's Law comes into play. Many of the problems I have seen have not occurred because the principal was knowingly trying to underpay commissions, but because no one ever really looked at the supporting documentation to ensure that the commission check was in the proper amount.

If sufficient information is provided with the commission statement so that each payment can be verified, the manufacturer's representative can do spot checks to satisfy himself that the commissions are being properly calculated. Further, I believe that if all the supporting documentation is attached it will be less likely for inadvertent errors to be made. It is under the circumstances of insufficient documentation being provided that a fertile breeding environment for errors is created. If the person calculating the commissions is unsure about an adjustment, and if the documentation isn't being provided, it makes it more likely that the uncertainty will be resolved in favor of the principal rather than the manufacturer's representative.

Failure to Object Can Be Used Against You

An argument which I have had to deal with on several occasions is as follows:

> The principal calculated commissions in this manner for several years and the manufacturer's representative knowingly accepted the payments without objection. Therefore, the manufacturer's representative has ratified the principal's method of

> calculating commissions and has waived any
> right to seek any underpayment.

This often makes a compelling practical argument, although generally it is legally deficient. If the contract specifies the manner of calculating commissions and the principal fails to follow that method, there would generally be no legal reason why the sales representative could not go back and recalculate the commissions and seek the balance owed. Most written manufacturer's representative agreements provide that the contracts can only be modified in writing and signed by the parties to the agreement. Typically there are no such written modifications to support these improper commission calculations.

Although there are generally significant legal problems from the principal's standpoint in justifying the underpayment of commissions in the event that there is a dispute which is subject to arbitration or mediation, this is typically the type of claim which is either significantly compromised or disregarded. In the circumstances in which it has arisen in my practice, it has been in conjunction with significant termination claims. In each instance we were awarded the termination commissions, but the arbitrators followed the principal's method of calculating commissions, even though it was not supported by the written contract. If the manufacturer's representative would have verified the proper payments during the course of the relationship, the problem may have been avoided.

Document Your Objections

If during the course of your relationship with your principal you discover that deductions are being taken from your commission payments which you do not believe are supportable by your contract, you should bring these to the attention of your principal as soon as possible. In some cases, your principal may feel justified in taking the deductions and will not agree to make any adjustments. The manufacturer's representative then is in somewhat of a dilemma. If he objects vehemently and insists upon a change, the result can be the termination of the relationship. This may end up costing the representative more money in the long run. If he does not object, it may be interpreted as a waiver.

The best thing to do under these circumstances is to object in writing to the improper commission calculations. Your principal may choose to ignore your comments and continue to calculate commissions the way it has done in the past. By making these written objections, however, you are laying the foundation to contest the underpayments at a later date. For example, if two or three years later your principal decides to terminate the relationship, you can always go back under those circumstances and contest the underpayments. In Michigan, for example, there is a six-year statute of limitations. This means that in the event of a termination you could contest underpayments for the six-year period preceding the termination.

Jack Ciupak and Associates v. First Inertia Switch, Ltd. --Revisited

As a general rule, every time I file a new commission lawsuit, I generally seek sales records for the three years prior to termination and perform an audit to ensure that the commissions prior to termination were properly paid. I will ordinarily do this even if my client believes that all of the pre-termination commissions had been properly paid. As indicated in Chapter Two, a few years ago I handled a claim for a client and his wife who became good friends of my wife and me. The agency was Jack Ciupak and Associates. At the time we filed the lawsuit, Jack Ciupak and Associates had a claim for commissions of approximately $1,000,000. Before we filed, I asked Jack and Bess whether there was any need to go back and verify the sales prior to termination to ensure that all commissions had been properly paid. Bess assured me that there was no problem with this, and that she carefully monitored the commission payments.

After we were in litigation for almost two years, we discovered that the defendant in this case, First Inertia Switch, Ltd., had not been calculating and paying commissions in accordance with the contract. As mentioned in Chapter Two, First Inertia Switch (FISL) made fuel cut-off switches which were sold to Ford Motor Company and were used to prevent the type of fires that occurred in the '70s and '80s when Pintos were rear-ended, causing the fuel tanks to catch fire and sometimes explode. FISL initially made the fuel cut-off switches in England and exported them to the United States. After a few years, a new plant was built in Grand

Blanc, Michigan, and the parts were manufactured in the Michigan plant.

We discovered that FISL had been subtracting freight, duty, and insurance costs which were incurred in shipping the parts to the United States for sale to Ford Motor Company. This was arguably justifiable under the written sales representative agreement when FISL was importing the parts from England. The problem is that once the parts began to be manufactured in Michigan, freight, duty, and insurance continued to be deducted. Further, we discovered that FISL was subtracting the commission from the piece price of the parts and paying a commission on the net remainder. We believed that these were improper deductions under the contract. We ended up filing a second lawsuit and resolved the pre-termination commission claim, but our position was weakened because the claim was not filed earlier.

Part of the problem was that Jack Ciupak and Associates was receiving monthly commissions of approximately $30,000 to $40,000. As with most small agencies, there is a limited amount of manpower, or womanpower in this case, and it is difficult to audit each month's commission statements. Further, when the relationship is going well, most salespeople do not like to rock the boat and create conflict where none apparently exists.

Renegotiating Your Commission Rate

One of the sure signs of success for a manufacturer's representative is the occasion when his principal wants to renegotiate the compensation provisions of the sales representation agreement. In some cases there may be a legitimate reason why the principal would want to take this action. Perhaps the customer is requiring price concessions, or there may be other problems beyond the control of the principal. In other circumstances, the principal may be attempting merely to increase profitability at the expense of the manufacturer's representative. It is important when addressing a commission reduction situation to attempt to determine what the true motivation of the principal is.

For purposes of this section, I will presume that the manufacturer's representative represents an automotive supplier who sells multiple parts to an automotive customer. These same principles, however, will apply to other industries.

Identify the Problem

Whenever your principal is seeking to reduce your commission rate, you should first attempt to obtain as much information as possible as to what the real problem is. In some cases, a manufacturer's representative will have access to enough accounting and cost information to be able to determine whether there is a profitability problem with a specific part or product line. Other manufacturer's representatives may be kept in the dark. It is important to obtain as much information as possible so that you can identify the problem before attempting to craft a solution. There may be a problem with an inaccurate estimate of the original cost to produce the parts, increased material costs, machine and equipment problems, etc. It is also important to determine whether the problem relates to a specific part or product line or is a more global problem. Until you and the principal have been able to agree upon what the problem is, it is very difficult to fashion a solution.

Create a Win/Win Result

Once you have identified the problem, you should then attempt to fashion a solution which addresses the specific problem. In attempting to fashion a solution, there are numerous considerations which must be taken into account and appropriately weighed. Some of these are as follows:

- As a team player, you should be willing to address and help to resolve your principal's problems. After all, solving other people's problems is what almost every salesperson does.

- Generally a manufacturer's representative is paid a percentage of the sales price, regardless of the amount of profit. If you are being asked to reduce your commission rate on low profit jobs, will your principal increase your commission rate on high profit jobs?

- Resist any attempt to institute a global solution for a provincial problem. If there is a problem with one particular part, you should not agree to let your principal use this as an excuse to institute an across the board commission reduction.

- Perhaps profit could be increased with manufacturing or efficiency changes. In some cases, a manufacturer's representative's expertise can help to resolve these types of problems. In other instances, outside help may be needed to increase efficiency.

- As a general rule, you should not give something up without getting something else in exchange. If you are able to agree on a commission reduction on one part, try to get an increase on a different part involving comparable dollars. Another alternative may be to increase the post-termination payout in exchange for a commission reduction. Try to avoid being put into the position of being a "victim." Victimization begets victimization.

- Don't allow the solution to outlive the problem. If you agree on a commission reduction, be sure that the reduction is limited to the specific part and that it ends if the circumstances change. Inertia can be a powerful force. It is generally very difficult to change back to a higher commission rate even when the problems giving rise to the lower rate are gone. You must be persistent. If the problem gets fixed, the commission rate should revert to the prior level.

- Generally it is never advisable to renegotiate the post-termination payout provision. Any time your principal wants to renegotiate the termination provision of your agreement to reduce the payout, you should be very concerned. By definition, the principal is considering terminating the relationship. If your principal wants to renegotiate the post-termination payout provision, then you must do an economic analysis calculating the termination commissions under the existing agreement and compare that to the post-termination commissions under the proposed new agreement. If there is a significant reduction, you should ask yourself, "What do I get in exchange for the reduced termination commissions?" Be careful, because statements like "We don't have any plans to terminate the agreement" or "Things are going well, we don't plan to make any changes" can be fool's gold.

In many of these types of negotiations, there will be an implied threat that if you do not agree to the new terms you will be terminated. My experience has been that a termination will likely happen in either event. You will generally be better protected if you are terminated under the old agreement than if you are terminated under the new agreement.

Confirm the Solution in Writing

Any time you negotiate a change to your manufacturer's representative agreement, whether the original agreement is in writing or oral, you should always confirm the change in writing. If the change is going to be for a limited time period, you should especially be sure to have any change confirmed in writing. Otherwise it is very easy for the change to go on indefinitely. Having the change confirmed in writing will also help to bring some closure to the situation.

4

Special Considerations

Eliminating Conflict of Interest Issues

One of the biggest problems a manufacturer's representative can face concerns the issue of conflict of interest. For many independent sales representative agencies who represent multiple principals, there can be both actual and potential conflicts. Under some circumstances, the existence of a conflict of interest by a manufacturer's representative can be used as a defense against the payment of commissions. For this reason, conflict of interest issues must be taken very seriously.

Potential Conflicts of Interest

A potential conflict of interest arises when a manufacturer's representative represents two principals who have the present capability to manufacture and sell products which may be competitive to each other. In some cases, the potentially competitive products may only involve a small percentage of the actual product sales and may not in fact constitute a problem for either principal.

A potential conflict of interest, however, is still a serious matter and should be addressed as discussed below.

Actual Conflicts of Interest

An actual conflict of interest exists when a manufacturer's representative is representing two principals who manufacture and sell competing products. This occurs when the representative has the ability to recommend to a customer one of two competing products which he represents. This is the most serious problem area.

Under almost no circumstances should a manufacturer's representative be in a position in which he can recommend or otherwise influence the selection of one of two competing products to a customer where he handles both products. Under these circumstances, it is difficult for the manufacturer's representative's own self-interests not to affect his recommendation, i.e., advocating the product under which he would get the highest commission rate. This would obviously affect the ability of the representative to be an effective advocate for each of his principals. This circumstance generally must be avoided at all times. Such a conflict of interest will invariably violate the implied, if not the express, terms of your contractual relationship.

Resolving Conflicts of Interest

My advice to the manufacturer's representatives whom I represent is that they must address all circumstances involving both potential and actual conflicts of interest. A representative should avoid even the appearance of impropriety.

I have on many occasions seen instances in which a principal was aware of a competing line that a manufacturer's representative handled, and it was never a problem during the term of the relationship because there was not an actual conflict. This can often change in the event of a termination, when some principals may seek to avoid the payment of a post-termination commission obligation. Suddenly conflicts which were not a problem during the term of the relationship become a big problem when it comes time for the representative to collect his termination commissions.

My advice to all of my manufacturer's representatives is that on an annual basis, they advise their principals of the other principals whom they represent and the product lines which they handle. First of all, if a principal is unhappy with the fact that a representative is carrying a possible competitor's product line, the issue can be directly addressed and perhaps an accommodation can be made. As a general rule, it is better to know if there will be a problem sooner rather than later.

There are often many ways to resolve these marginal conflicts without the necessity of giving up one of the lines. Perhaps one or two accounts could be handled by the principal as a house account. Another possible example would be that the representative would agree not to handle a particular product for one of the principals.

It is important for these issues to be addressed head-on, before they result in significant dissatisfaction on behalf of the principal. There are two key reasons for this. First of all, the manufacturer's representative should want to maintain a good relationship with his principal. This is accomplished by having open and honest communication. If the principal has a legitimate concern, it should be directly addressed by the representative.

The second reason is that an actual conflict of interest can jeopardize the ability of the manufacturer's representative to recover commissions. Such a conflict of interest can be a breach of the representative's express or implied duties and obligations to his principal. The most significant defense to a conflict of interest claim is consent by the principal. If on an annual basis the manufacturer's representative notifies all of his principals of the other principals represented and their product lines, it is very difficult for a principal to raise conflict of interest as a defense against the payment of commissions after a termination. Most conflict of interest claims can be defeated by establishing two factors: (1) knowledge by the principal of the existence of the conflict, as a result of disclosure by the manufacturer's representative; and (2) consent to the potential or actual conflict by the principal.

It is important to remember that notifying a principal of the other principals and product lines represented should be done in a positive manner. In this regard, a manufacturer's representative should keep in mind that he is selling at all times. This disclosure can and should be used as an opportunity to promote the representative and the other lines which he carries. It should be remembered that one of the advantages of carrying multiple lines is the synergistic effect that the multiple lines can have upon all of the products which are sold by each principal. For example, a buyer may call a manufacturer's representative to discuss a specific product. During the course of the conversation, the representative can use that contact as an opportunity to sell complementary product lines. This often will give a principal exposure for which it may not otherwise have had an opportunity.

In addition to being important to maintain good relations with your principal, the disclosure of your other principals and product lines on an annual basis will also help to effectively eliminate the ability of one of your principals to attempt to avoid the payment of commissions in the event of a termination based upon some feigned dissatisfaction with other product lines.

Representing Companies Owned by Native Americans

Many Native Americans or Indian tribes have made many millions of dollars in legalized gambling. Some tribes have decided to attempt to diversify their businesses and have gotten into manufacturing. As a result of the federal government's emphasis on minority content, especially in the automotive industry, there has been a significant trend toward manufacturing enterprises owned by Native Americans. There can be some significant drawbacks, however, in representing businesses owned by Native Americans because they are considered to be sovereign entities. This means that ordinarily an Indian tribe cannot be sued in either a state or federal court unless there is a clear and unequivocal waiver of sovereign immunity. Thus, in order to pursue any legal claim for commissions, absent a waiver of sovereign immunity, you must resort to suing in the tribal court.

Ernest I. Young v Sault Ste. Marie Tribe of Chippewa Indians

I recently represented a client named Ernest I. Young in a series of claims against the Sault Ste. Marie Tribe of Chippewa Indians. Young owned a small plastic injection molding manufacturing company called Special Plastic Products Corporation. He is a Native American and also a member of the Sault Ste. Marie Tribe of Chippewa Indians.

In 1994, Young and his company, SPP, entered into a Joint Venture Agreement with the tribe. In exchange for a fifty percent stake in the company, the tribe contributed approximately $1,000,000 and committed to loan an additional $1,000,000. SPP at the time had sales of approximately $9,000,000 and was a certified minority supplier to the automotive industry.

Although the Joint Venture Master Agreement only obligated the tribe to contribute the $1,000,000 loan and an additional $1,000,000 in capital, Young was told that if he obtained new business, the tribe would provide the necessary financing. Based upon this understanding, Mr. Young began a concerted effort to obtain a substantial amount of new business. He was successful in securing a purchase order from General Motors for the new GM T800 program to provide a cowl vent assembly.[21] The GM T800 program is the full-sized pick-up body for the Suburban and related vehicles. This would have generated new sales of at least $15,000,000 per year, likely for a period of five to ten years. The total value of the contract would likely have exceeded $100,000,000.

Unfortunately, the tooling and other startup costs far exceeded the $2,000,000 committed by the tribe. In September of 1996, the tribe decided that it was going to put no further money into the venture. Mr. Young's employment was terminated; the tribe told General Motors it didn't want the business; and the tribe closed down SPP and liquidated the assets. Mr. Young went from being the owner of a successful minority automotive supplier to being unemployed in a matter of a few months.

We filed two lawsuits which were ultimately dismissed based upon sovereign immunity and the fact that there was an arbitration provision in the contracts. In February of 1998, we arbitrated the breach of contract claims. The

---

[21] The cowl vent is the vented plastic part between the windshield and hood.

tort claims could only have been pursued in Tribal Court. Since the chief judge of the Tribal Court was one of the defendants in one of the lawsuits, I felt that our chances of a successful result in Tribal Court were slim to none. Further, it appeared to me that the chief/chairman of the tribe likely had significant influence over the Tribal Court.

After an arbitration lasting approximately three days, we obtained an award of $546,000 for breach of the employment agreement, but nothing for the destruction of the business. The tribe appealed the arbitration award to the Michigan Court of Appeals.

On May 11, 2001, the Michigan Court of Appeals affirmed the Trial Court's confirmation of the arbitration award. The Court of Appeals also agreed with our position that Mr. Young was entitled to 12% interest on the arbitration award pursuant to the Michigan's Judgment Interest Statute.[22] The arbitration award with interest totaled $746,630 as of May 11, 2001. Refusing to give up, the tribe through their attorneys filed an Application For Leave to Appeal with the Michigan Supreme Court on June 1, 2001. On March 4, 2002, we received notification from the Michigan Supreme Court that the tribe's Application For Leave to Appeal was denied.[23] After being turned down by three courts, on June 3, 2002, the tribe filed an Application For Writ of

---

[22] *Young v. Sault Ste. Marie Tribe*, No. 214136 (Mich. App., May 11, 2001).

[23] *Young v. Sault Ste. Marie Tribe*, No. 119364 (Mich., March 4, 2002).

Certiorari with the United States Supreme Court. We filed our response with the United States Supreme Court on July 7, 2002. On October 7, 2002, we received notification from the United States Supreme Court that the tribe's application was denied.[24] On December 17, 2002, we received payment from the tribe totaling $912,151.05. This was almost five years after the arbitration had concluded.[25]

This is an example of the amount of time it can sometimes take to obtain closure to litigation. The claim in this case has been pending for six years and out-of-pocket expenses for our office, and necessarily for Mr. Young, have exceeded $65,000.

Mr. Young would have been much better off if he had never made the deal with the tribe. The point here is that the rules are substantially different for Indian tribes. In general, tribes cannot be sued without their permission other than in Tribal Court. Be very cautious in entering into any business relationships with an Indian tribe. At a minimum, be sure that you have a waiver of sovereign immunity and that you can resolve your disputes either in arbitration or in non-tribal courts.

---

[24] *Sault Ste. Marie Tribe v. Young*, 123 S.Ct. 100 (2002).

[25] As of July of 2003, the case was still not 100% completed. The tribe chose to file an appeal with regard to the amount of interest it was ordered to pay by the court. If they continue to pursue this appeal, this case will be pending for probably another 3-4 years. Fortunately, my client now has been paid.

In negotiating a sales representative agreement with a Native American tribe, it is important to have a provision in the contract which contains a clear and unequivocal waiver of sovereign immunity. Often this is coupled with an agreement to arbitrate. I would not recommend entering into a sales representation agreement with any manufacturing company owned by a Native American tribe without a waiver of sovereign immunity.

5

Be Aware: Forewarned is Forearmed

Beware of the New Sales Manager

There are several warning signs of future problems in your relationship with your principal or employer. One of these is a new sales manager. This is especially true when a principal has primarily used independent manufacturer's representatives and has decided to hire a sales manager to oversee the representatives. This can often be a precursor to the replacement of you and the other manufacturer's representatives and the implementation of a direct sales force.

Often the sales manager will want you to take him along on your sales calls. This can lead to the sales manager, and other representatives of your principal, meeting directly with your buyers and customers without you. This may appear very innocent at first, and in some cases it is innocent. It can have a tendency, however, to create a direct relationship which can make your position as manufacturer's representative or independent salesperson vulnerable.

In some instances, the conflict between the sales manager and the independent manufacturer's representatives can be very direct and hostile. I have seen instances in which representatives have been able to cause a principal to change his mind and fire a new sales manager. In one particular instance, the manufacturer's representatives said that they clearly could not work with the new sales manager and one of them had to go. If this type of a confrontation is going to occur, it must occur when you are in the strongest position, i.e., before the sales manager has had an opportunity to establish a direct relationship with your customers and make it possible for you to be replaced. Listen to your intuition. If you believe that a problem is brewing, you are generally correct.

This is not to say that any time there is a new sales manager you must give your principal an ultimatum that either the sales manager must go or you must go. It is merely another potential problem area you must be aware of. Remember that your principal will act in his own economic interest. Try to make sure that it is to your principal's economic interest to retain you.

Beware of the Consultant

There seems to be a trend for manufacturing companies, as well as many other companies, to hire consultants to either increase profitability or try to otherwise improve the financial condition of the company. In many cases, this seems to be incidental to a plan to market the company. Generally, the consultants have an accounting background and almost never a sales background. One area which is sure to get close scrutiny any time a consultant is hired is the sales commissions paid to a manufacturer's representative or employee salesperson.

You can assume that one of the economic evaluations which will be made will be the level of sales commissions paid compared to the cost of an in-house sales staff. Looking strictly at the numbers, it may appear to be difficult to justify the commissions compared to the cost of an employee or employees. Generally, this occurs when the business is at a more mature stage, but it can also occur during a period of significant growth. The consultant will be asking the owner if the value of the manufacturer's representative can be justified compared to the cost of a direct sales force.

Obviously, these types of evaluations can be very shortsighted. I personally believe that commissioned salespeople are better motivated and, therefore, will obtain better results than salaried salespeople. It is often difficult to disregard the short-term benefits of a reduction in the sales expense, however, even though there may be significant long-term negative consequences in the form of decreased future sales.[26]

Be prepared to justify the value which you bring or your organization brings to the relationship. This can include personal relationships with key purchasing personnel involved, more detailed knowledge of market conditions, unique customer requirements, market trends, etc.

---

[26] This can often occur years after the consultant has been paid.

Be careful about disclosing too many of the details of your contacts and knowledge of future customer requirements, projects, or programs. Sometimes this information will be used against you.

This is not to indicate that you should be an obstructionist. Try to be positive and contributing, but also be wary that the consultant may be looking to eliminate your role. The consultant's objective will be to improve the financial condition of the company. The easiest and "no-brainer" way to do this is to either reduce or eliminate the commission expense. Keep in mind that the consultant will be attempting to justify his or her cost. You will likely be a key target.

Danger Sign: Making More Money Than Your Boss/Principal

It is common knowledge in the sales business that you are in jeopardy any time you are making more money than the person you are reporting to. There are compensation hierarchies within business organizations and between manufacturer's representatives and their principals. The hierarchy is disrupted whenever a salesperson's compensation is higher than it is expected to be.

I recently took the deposition of a vice president of sales in a case involving a claim by three employee sales representatives against their former employer for sales commissions related to the sale of computer software programs. The vice president testified that there were target income amounts for the sales representatives' positions. He also testified that on one occasion in which a sales representative was paid more money than the sales manager, the sales manager vehemently complained to him. Of the three claims we had, two of them involved retroactive increases in quotas and another involved reneging on a compensation plan modification.

It has been my experience that compensation decisions by many companies are often very result-oriented. Many compensation decisions are essentially "backed into." This means that a decision is first made as to how much money a salesperson should make, often even after the close of the fiscal year. Decisions are then made and compensation plans adjusted to make sure the salesperson makes no more than what management believes that position is worth. If the salesperson does not agree to these changes and continues to object to them, normally we can be successful in obtaining the compensation originally agreed upon. Unfortunately, termination of the employment is generally the result of these compensation disputes. Most people, however, don't want to work for a company which will not follow its own compensation plan.

There is no doubt in my mind that, as a general rule, if you are being paid more money than your manager or principal, the circumstances will generally be short-lived. If you want the relationship to continue, you will need to be sensitive to this fact of life and be prepared to deal with it. Be prepared to be an advocate for your position, remembering that although you may be making more money in a particular year, you probably sacrificed in prior years to be in the position you are in now. There are always other arguments you can make to support your position. Be prepared to do this.

Expect to Be Terminated

Whether your relationship with your principal or employer is going very well or very badly, you should always have an exit strategy. You must regularly give thought and consideration to what you would do if you were terminated on very short notice. Do you have skills which are easily transferable to another arena? Have you signed a non-competition agreement which will effectively take you out of the industry for a period of time? Do you have skills which are marketable? Have you ever prepared a resume? Have you ever attempted to market test your value? Always plan ahead.

As indicated earlier and as suggested by Robert Ringer in his book *Looking Out For Number One* (Fawcett Crest, New York), one of the best ways to achieve a positive result is by planning and preparing for negative consequences. Perhaps you should have an interview with a headhunter who is knowledgeable in your industry. This is not to say that you need to tell him or her that you are planning on leaving or changing your employment, but it is always a good idea to have some of those contacts made in advance so that you know where to go if and when a termination should occur. Further, you may find that you are being underpaid for your position and you may find a better job. We all know that loyalty to employees is not what it was twenty years ago. It seems to be becoming a thing of the past. You should be prepared to be as flexible as possible to be successful in today's marketplace.

Don't Spend All of Your Money!

Many of us, salespersons or otherwise, have a tendency to live at the maximum level of our income. This is especially dangerous for commissioned salespersons. Most employment relationships, and, in fact, most sales representation agreements, can be terminated at any time for any reason. I generally take the position in negotiating a sales representation agreement that the agreement can be terminated at any time as long as the principal pays my client for the business which he obtained. For employee salespersons or manufacturer's representatives with a limited number of principals, termination and the stoppage of commissions can be a very devastating event.

I have had several instances in which we were forced to substantially compromise commission claims because my client was not in a position economically to wage a long commission battle. I generally recommend that salespeople live relatively conservatively. You should always attempt to put money away to sustain a long legal battle.

On the average, most cases that settle after litigation is commenced do not settle for approximately one year. This is in part because we ordinarily have to undertake some discovery to properly quantify the claim. If the case goes to trial, it can take, on average, two years from the date of filing to have a jury trial. If we are successful and the defendant appeals, the matter can be tied up in the Court of Appeals for an additional two to four years. There can then be an additional delay of another year if the defendant files an Application for Leave to Appeal to the state Supreme Court. If the application is accepted, which is unlikely, it can take another one to two years to obtain a decision.

You should always assume that you will be terminated. Try to have enough money to last for at least one to two years without any additional income. If you are an independent manufacturer's representative, it may take that long to locate a new principal and obtain new business which will generate commissions.

It is particularly important for salespeople to save for that rainy day. There is a significant probability that it will occur.

Trust Your Instincts

As the human race has become more evolved and more civilized, we may have become, in my opinion, overly rational and analytical. Sometimes this is a good thing and sometimes it is not. Thousands of years ago, when our forefathers lived in caves, they were much more reliant upon their instincts than we are today. Many times we will get a "bad feeling" about a person, a circumstance, a place, etc. Our rational mind tends to take over and we then rationalize away this "bad feeling," whether it be a fear, anxiety, or apprehension. It has been my experience that I am generally better off following my instinct and intuition rather than rationalizing or explaining it away. If you are concerned that there are problems in your relationship with your employer or principal, even if they are difficult to explain or pinpoint, they are probably real. If you believe that you are vulnerable to a termination, then you probably are. Use these occasions as opportunities to be vigilant and to prepare yourself for negative consequences. Most likely they will occur and probably sooner rather than later.

6

Termination

It's Not the Money — It's the Amount

The lines of demarcation between the end of one stage of your sales representation relationship and the beginning of another stage are not always clear. In most instances, the boundaries are not easily discernable and the lines are drawn in shades of gray.

As indicated earlier, there are several warning signs that your sales representative relationship may be in jeopardy. Some of these are as follows:

- Making more money in commissions than your employer or principal believes the position is worth

- Making more money than your contact person, i.e., sales manager or owner in a small company

- A termination payout provision which creates an economic incentive to terminate your services

- A new sales manager

- A consultant

- Any change in ownership. This is especially true if the assets and business of your principal are being purchased by an existing company with an existing in-house sales force

- A sudden interest in more of the details of your day-to-day activities, including detailed call reports and requests by your principal or your sales manager to accompany you on sales calls

- Direct contact between your principal or employer and your customers without your knowledge or consent

These are all potential problem areas. Again, it is important to emphasize that you should listen to your intuition. If your intuition tells you that a problem is brewing, then this feeling should not be discounted. Do not stick your head in the sand and hope that the problem either never arises or eventually goes away. The chances are that it will arise and that it will not go away.

It is important to keep in mind two relatively simple truths whenever you have a problem getting paid commissions you have earned. The first is: "It's business—it's not personal."

The likely reason you are not being paid is not because your boss or principal doesn't like you, you are too old, the wrong sex, wrong race, wrong national origin, overweight, or any other similarly personal reason. In almost all cases, it is because of the economics. This leads to the second truth which is really a corollary to the first: "It's not the money — it's the amount." Your principal or employer does not have a problem in principle in paying money to you. He just doesn't want to pay you the *amount* of money you have earned.

If you assume that all business decisions are motivated by dollars and cents, you will be correct 99.5% of the time. I have always believed it is somewhat demeaning for a salesperson to look for other reasons for their problems with not getting paid. One of the reasons this happens, in my opinion, is because I believe salespeople take a failure to pay so personally that they can't believe the underlying motivation is so simplistic.

They seem to say, "It can't be just the amount of money — there has to be something more." The salesperson will then start to look for other reasons: "I'm too old." "I'm a woman." "I'm a black man (or woman)." "I'm overweight.", etc. Whenever a salesperson dwells on one of these other factors, the affect associated with the failure to pay or termination become significantly heightened. There is more stress, anxiety, bitterness, and negative emotion in general. This results in greater trauma.

You must treat your commission problem like any other business problem. The first step in solving any problem is to define the problem. If you define it as being your sex, your race, your age, your weight, etc., then the problem becomes almost unsolvable. If you recognize that the problem is "not the money but the amount", it is much easier to address the problem, formulate a solution, and then move on. This is especially true if you seek the assistance of a lawyer in solving your problem.

It is not realistic to believe that your principal or employer will ever admit either of the following, even after they lose:

> "I was wrong," or
> "The decision not to pay you was based upon your race." (Or sex, age, weight, or a similarly legally proscribed reason.)

A case I was involved in when I was completing this book is a good example. This is the case of *Tech Interface, Inc. v. The Andrew Corporation*. The sales representation agreement contained an arbitration provision mandating arbitration through the American Arbitration Association. We filed a Demand For Arbitration and also filed a lawsuit in the Federal District Court for the Eastern District of Michigan, Southern Division. (See footnote 27 on page 116 for an explanation of the reason for the filing of both an arbitration claim and a federal lawsuit.)

The Andrew Corporation manufactured cellular phone antenna assemblies primarily for use with the General Motors OnStar™ System. Andrew Corporation's largest customer was General Motors.

In the early years of the contract, there was little demand for the cellular antenna assemblies manufactured by The Andrew Corporation and its predecessor, The Antenna Company. The sales representation agreement was signed in 1991. From 1991 through 1995, total sales were approximately $1.3 million and total commissions were approximately $72,000. In 1996, annual sales reached the $1 million mark for the first time. In approximately 1999, General Motors decided to expand its OnStar™ System. The OnStar™ System uses cellular phones in conjunction with a global positioning system. Beginning in the 2000 model year, General Motors made the OnStar™ System available on virtually every vehicle it manufactures.

Sales increased from approximately $1 million in 1996 to almost $20 million in 2000. The sales representation agreement provided for a 5% commission. At $20 million in sales, this is $1 million in annual commissions. Projected sales for 2001, 2002, and 2003 were expected to climb to approximately $25 million per year.

In the fall of 2000, my client was informed that the sales representation agreement would have to be renegotiated because "too much money was budgeted for commissions." Obviously my client was not very thrilled with this revelation. In November of 2000, The Andrew Corporation stopped paying all commissions to Tech Interface. In my opinion, this action was taken to pressure the sales agency into renegotiating a contract more favorable to The Andrew Corporation.

My client in this case believed if we merely demonstrated to The Andrew Corporation that Tech Interface had done all of the work it was required to do under the clear language of the manufacturer's representative agreement, that The Andrew Corporation would agree Tech Interface should be paid its commissions. What my client failed to realize, however, was that this is not an issue of right or wrong. The Andrew Corporation had no problem in principle with paying commissions; it just did not want to pay the *amount* of the commissions which were owed to Tech Interface. This was a difficult concept for one of the two partners of Tech Interface to grasp, because he felt the obligation to pay should have been crystal clear. Although I could never prove this, I believe that The Andrew Corporation had determined the amount of commissions it wanted to pay and attempted to find a justification to back into the result it wanted.[27]

---

[27] We settled this case a few months after the arbitration and Federal Court proceedings were filed for commissions which will total approximately $3.7 million based upon current projections. It is unusual for there to be an arbitration proceeding and a court proceeding pending between the same parties at the same time regarding the same contract. This was a strategic decision I made that was calculated to put the maximum amount of pressure on The Andrew Corporation in two forums.

The manufacturer's representative agreement between the parties contained a list of specific customers. One of the customers was General Motors. For the first few years of the OnStar™ program, all of the components for the antennas were shipped directly to General Motors. The antenna assembly was installed by General Motors personnel. As the program began to expand, however, General Motors made the decision to shift some of the assembly operations to its suppliers. The bases, which are affixed to the inside and outside of the rear window or back light, were shipped to the glass companies who supplied the windshield and rear window. The cable which connects the antenna to the cellular phone in the vehicle was shipped to the wiring harness company. The mast was shipped to General Motors, who would have the dealer personnel install the mast upon delivery.

Most of the wiring harnesses were shipped to Delphi

Most commission problems do not have their genesis in failure but in success. It is much more likely that the problem has arisen because you significantly *exceeded*

---

which, just a short time before, split off from General Motors. General Motors was on the customer list. Delphi and the glass companies were not on the customer list. Andrew Corporation took the position that since Delphi and the glass companies were not on the customer list, no commissions were therefore owed on those sales. In fact, Andrew argued that it had overpaid commissions by approximately $500,000 on sales to customers not on the customer list and stated they wanted those commissions repaid to them.

Since the manufacturer's representative agreement contained a mandatory arbitration clause, we filed a Demand For Arbitration with the American Arbitration Association seeking unpaid commissions for those customers specifically identified on the customer list. Since Andrew was taking the position that customers who were not included on the customer list were not covered by the manufacturer's representative agreement, we filed a separate action in Federal Court in Michigan seeking "life of part" commissions for sales to those customers.

In its answer to the Federal Court action, Andrew filed a Motion to Dismiss the court proceeding based upon the arbitration agreement. Unfortunately for Andrew, this placed the company in somewhat of a Catch-22 position. In order to argue that the Federal Court proceeding should be dismissed, it essentially had to acknowledge that the sales to the customers not on the customer list were covered by the arbitration agreement. If they were covered by the arbitration agreement, then there was no defense to the payment of commissions. This particular contract required commissions be paid for four years after termination.

Federal District Judge Julian Abele Cook, Jr., denied Andrew's motion to dismiss the case. Instead, Judge Cook stayed the proceedings pending the outcome of the arbitration. The case was settled shortly thereafter.

expectations. The *amount* of money you have earned has created the problem. It may be hard to think of your predicament this way, but you should be proud of the fact that you are in this position, because it is an affirmation of your skill and competency as a salesperson. This may be a tough sell to your wife or husband when the commission payments stop, but it is generally a true fact.

The benefit of recognizing these truths is that there will be a significant reduction in the anxiety you will experience because of your commission problem. You now have an answer to the following questions:

- "Why did this happen to me?"
- "What did I do wrong?"

The answers generally are, "Because I am very good at what I do," and "I did nothing wrong."

Hopefully by following some of the recommendations in this book, you will be able to minimize the probability of commission problems and the resultant angst.

The Sale of Your Principal's/Employer's Business

You must accept the proposition that your position is in jeopardy any time the assets or business of either your principal or your employer are in the process of being sold. Commissioned salespeople are especially vulnerable under these circumstances. It is my belief that one of the principal selling points in the acquisition of a company is the amount of commission money that can be saved by acquiring a manufacturing company's assets and business. Generally, the plan is to merge the sales activity into the existing sales force of the acquiring company and to terminate the sales force of the acquired company. The commission savings goes straight to the bottom line and profits are generally realized almost immediately. If your sales representation agreement does not have a provision which renders the acquiring company liable for the commission obligations under your contract, you may have a significant problem. See Chapter Two on how to address this problem in your sales representation agreement. The time to address this problem is long before it occurs.

Oral sales representation agreements can create some interesting scenarios when the principal sells its assets. I have been involved in several lawsuits in which there were either oral agreements or expired written agreements in existence at the time of an acquisition. One such instance was in the case of *Darryl Plimpton v McCurdy Manufacturing Company.* McCurdy was a medium-sized stamping company selling metal stampings and assemblies to the automotive manufacturers, including, specifically, Ford Motor Company. Darryl Plimpton was an employee and had an oral agreement with McCurdy that he would be paid a 1% commission on any business he was responsible for obtaining. The McCurdy Company was courted by Masco Tech, a subsidiary of Masco Industries. Ultimately, a sale of the assets took place.

Ordinarily, whenever a manufacturing company enters into an agreement to sell its stock or assets, there are certain representations and warranties made by the seller. One of these is typically the requirement for the disclosure of any contractual obligations or agreements which can not be terminated upon thirty days notice. In the *Darryl Plimpton* matter, Mr. McCurdy apparently believed that Darryl Plimpton had a written agreement which provided for little or no commissions in the event of a termination. Alternatively, if Mr. McCurdy believed there was no written agreement, he was not familiar with the Procuring Cause Doctrine in Michigan, which created the possibility of a commission entitlement, even in the event of a termination or acquisition.

Although Darryl Plimpton and Mr. McCurdy were close friends, I suspect that it was made known to Mr. McCurdy that he faced exposure to Masco in the event that Darryl Plimpton was entitled to continuing commissions from McCurdy Manufacturing, now Masco Tech. Mr. McCurdy was not as helpful as Darryl thought he might have been. Darryl worked extremely hard and was very successful. Through his efforts, McCurdy obtained approximately $40 million in annual new business. This is one of the reasons why the McCurdy Manufacturing Company was an attractive acquisition. That $40 million in annual sales was likely to be in production for approximately five years; thus, it was about $200 million in total sales for the life of parts.

After Masco purchased McCurdy's assets, Masco offered Darryl Plimpton a salaried position with the elimination of commissions. Since Darryl's commissions were going to total approximately $400,000 per year, which was approximately double the salary offered, the prospect was not very attractive.

Unfortunately, in Darryl's case, at the time of the acquisition he signed an arbitration agreement incidental to some stock options with Masco requiring mandatory arbitration through a national arbitration association.[28] Although we were able to obtain an arbitration award of $875,000, I felt that Masco had gotten off too inexpensively. In fact, I expect that Masco was quite satisfied with the result.

In this particular case, I was not happy with the arbitration panel. This was one of the instances in which we were provided with a list of commercial arbitrators and were able to strike up to three on the list. The arbitrators who were not struck by either side were then eligible to be appointed. Our panel consisted of a small business owner, an insurance company defense attorney, and the chairperson, who was an attorney who practiced law out of his home. This was not the type of panel which was likely to issue a seven-figure award to my client. I suspected that none of the arbitrators had ever earned more than $100,000 in any given year. In this case, I was asking them to award approximately $3,000,000 to my client. Further, I doubted that any of them were familiar with the automotive industry insofar as it related to commissions on production parts.

---

[28] Please see Chapter Two on my views of mandatory arbitration. These were in large part shaped by the *Darryl Plimpton* case.

Although I earned an attorney fee of approximately $279,000, I was quite disappointed with the results. My client should have received more.

The lessons which can be learned from the *Plimpton* case for a sales representative are:

- Don't rely on the fact that you have had a close personal relationship with your principal. You must expect that even your friends will act to further their own economic interests.

- Whenever possible, avoid mandatory arbitration through a national arbitration association, especially when you have little control over the selection of the arbitrators.

Should You Quit or Wait to Be Fired?

If your principal or employer wants to terminate you, often they will make your working life miserable to try to get you to quit. You must resist the urge to quit whenever possible. As a general rule, your claim for commissions will be stronger if you are terminated rather than if you quit. [29]

---

[29] In fact, many sales representative agreements provide for post-termination commissions only in the event of an involuntary termination of the sales representative. In any sales representation agreement I am involved in negotiating, I try to ensure that the post-termination commissions apply irrespective of whether the termination was initiated by the sales representative or by the principal.

The efforts by principals or employers to get you to quit can take many different forms. I have seen this happen on numerous occasions. Not coincidentally, it typically happens to those salespeople who have been very successful in generating new business which creates substantial commission exposure to their principal or employer.

The situation is generally different for manufacturer's representatives than employees. I will address each separately.

- **Manufacturer's representatives**: Principals typically have less control over the manufacturer's representative than employers have over employees. I have seen the following tactics used by principals against their manufacturer's representatives trying to get them to quit:

    ➢ Unexplained and unauthorized deductions from commission statements;

    ➢ Unilateral changes to commission rates or elimination of commissions as to certain accounts or projects; and

    ➢ Letters critical of performance in an attempt to lay a framework for termination.

- **Employee sales representatives:** Some of the examples I have seen used on my clients to pressure them to quit have included:

  ➢ Memos or e-mail critical of the salesperson's performance. These are generally used to create a record in the personnel file to support a case for termination;

  ➢ Negative performance evaluations. This is especially true regarding the subjective components of the evaluation. As far as I am concerned, sales performance, i.e., sales dollars, is the only true measure of a salesperson's performance; and

  ➢ Transfer from a sales position to nonsales position. This is usually the kiss of death. Good salespeople do not perform as well in nonsales positions without incentive compensation.

One of the first steps in attempting to deal effectively with the situation in which your principal/employer is attempting to get you to quit is to be able to identify that this is what is occurring. Try not to get too wrapped up in the emotion of the circumstances occurring at the time. You should try to take a step back and ask, "Why is my principal/employer doing this"? Is there a legitimate employer/principal concern, or are they attempting to get me to quit?"

In order to answer this question, a simple economic exercise is usually helpful. Write down three numbers. The first is your income last year; the second is your expected income this year; the third is your expected income next year. If there is significant increase in the second and third number, especially if you will be making more than your manager/principal, you should assume your principal/employer is trying to get you to quit. Again, this is because of the *amount* of the commissions you have earned or will earn. If you believe this is the case, you should see a lawyer immediately who is experienced in dealing with sales commission disputes. Remember, these decisions are almost always motivated strictly by economics.

The advice I typically give to my clients under these circumstances is that any time your principal/employer takes any action which violates your agreement, or with which you are otherwise in disagreement, you should express your disagreement in writing as soon as possible (see Chapter Three). In composing a written response to any such action, follow these guidelines:

- Be factual and unemotional. Address the specific issue or complaint and make a well-reasoned and factually supported response. Avoid sarcasm or any other negative emotion such as anger, hostility, etc.

- Do not send the letter immediately. Put it aside and review it in twenty-four hours.

- When you look at your letter after twenty-four hours, make any necessary corrections and then review it again in another twenty-four hours.

- Have your lawyer review the letter. *Do not let the lawyer write the letter.* It is usually easy to determine whether the letter is written by a lawyer or a lay person.

- If the letter is going to be mailed, send it first class and not certified mail. It is not necessary to send the letter certified and it will likely increase the chances it will be referred to a lawyer.

- Assume a judge, jury, or arbitrator will read your response one to two years later.

There is a very fine line to be walked in composing the letter. You want to express your disapproval, but you do not generally want to make it so strong that it causes your termination. In many cases, however, termination may be unavoidable.

The letter should lay the foundation for the theme which ultimately will be presented to a judge, jury, or arbitration panel: you did the work and you should be paid.

Termination Meetings: Don't Agree to Anything, Don't Sign Anything

When it comes to the time that you are meeting with the human resources director of your employer or any representative of your principal to discuss your termination, as a general rule you should never agree to anything or sign anything during that meeting. Listen to what the proposal is, obtain a copy in writing if possible, and then indicate that you must think about it. If you have not already done so, you must then contact a lawyer immediately to obtain an accurate evaluation of your legal position. Ordinarily, if you make an oral agreement or written agreement in that meeting to settle your claim, you will have to presume that the agreement will be enforceable. Although there are certain circumstances under which such an agreement may not be enforceable, you must assume that it will be enforceable.

It is usually very difficult to avoid settlement agreements. One tactic I have recommended for independent manufacturer's representatives who have partners is that only one partner should ever attend a termination meeting. This gives the salesperson the excuse that he must clear any agreement with his partner. If you are an employee, you should still think of an excuse to avoid a decision at the time. Tell your employer or your principal that you need to discuss the matter with your spouse, or give any other reason, but generally do not decide at that time. No decision should be made regarding commissions when you are first told you are being terminated.

This is not to say that you should not attempt to work out an amicable resolution with your employer or principal, but you owe it to yourself to be sure that it is a fair deal. You should contact a lawyer who can accurately evaluate your claim. This will allow you to make a reasoned decision as to whether the agreement makes economic sense. A few extra days should not make any difference if your principal/employer really wants to make a deal.

Document All Meetings and Conversations

When you are in the termination stage of your relationship, it is important to document all meetings and conversations. Write confirming letters regarding any discussions with your principal or employer concerning the issues of termination, payment of commission on disputed business, and virtually any other significant issue. If you are vigilant, you can control the record. This goes back to the story of the three umpires (see page 72). When you control the record, you have the ability to put your own spin on the events. This can be important two or three years down the road when you are attempting to establish your case in court.

It is especially important at this time that you have good legal counsel. At this stage of the relationship, I generally ask my clients to send to me copies of all correspondence they either send to or receive from their employer or principal. I ordinarily help them compose the communication in such a way as to put their claim in the best possible position. Again, I generally do not draft these letters for my clients. I prefer for my clients to put everything in their own words as much as possible. I then review the letter to be sure that all of the appropriate points are covered.

I want the correspondence during this stage of the relationship to lay the foundation for the theme or themes I will want to argue to a judge, jury, or arbitration panel in the future. These generally include the following:

- The reason you are being terminated is because your employer or principal is not willing to pay you the commissions you earned in accordance with your agreement, i.e., *greed.*

- The termination has nothing to do with the quality of your performance. In fact, you are being terminated for being too successful, i.e., *greed.*

It is important for the employer, and eventually the judge or jury reading these letters, to have the impression that it is the salesperson's words and not a lawyer's words. In fact, I will often let some spelling, punctuation, and grammatical errors go uncorrected.

If you are receiving legal advice at this time, *do not disclose that fact.* This will only ensure that your employer/principal gets his lawyer involved. Your principal/employer's lawyer may then be able to correct some mistakes which your principal/employer may otherwise make. Your principal/employer's lawyer may be involved anyway, but a sure way to guarantee that they will be involved is by letting your principal/employer know that your lawyer is involved.

Contacting Customers After Termination: To Do or Not to Do?

One question which is frequently asked of me by a sales representative after he has been terminated is, "What type of contact should I have with customers?" In part, this depends on whether there was an agreement or covenant not to compete executed during the term of your employment. Agreements not to compete are generally enforceable, provided they are reasonable in duration and area and reasonably related to a legitimate employer interest. You should presume that any covenant not to compete will be enforceable. You should also have the agreement reviewed by a competent lawyer.

Aside from considerations related to agreements or covenants not to compete, I generally recommend that my clients remain in contact with their customers. Often a phone call or short letter is a good way to accomplish this.

First of all, you must keep in mind that as a salesperson you are always selling. If you were successful in your prior position, you will likely be successful in your new position. Additionally, it is almost always advisable to maintain a good relationship with your prior customers. There are two key reasons for this. First of all, you may be calling upon them for a new principal or employer and you never want to burn any bridges. Additionally, you may be calling upon them to testify for you in the event of litigation. I generally prefer to have the customers hear about a termination from my client rather than from their employer or principal. An example of a written communication for an employee can be as follows:

Sample Letter

A-1 Customer
Anywhere, U.S.A.

Dear Customer:

I wanted to advise you that my employment with ABC Manufacturing Company was recently terminated. Although I will not be representing ABC any longer, I wanted to let you know that I have enjoyed working with you and hopefully I will be able to do so again.

I would also ask that you feel free to contact me at any time if there is anything which I can ever do. I would be happy to answer any questions or take any other action which would make the transition run smoothly.

Please feel free to contact me at any time.

Very truly yours,

Expert Salesperson

If you are an independent manufacturer's representative representing multiple lines, you should use this as an opportunity to sell your other principals' products. For example, the following letter may be appropriate:

Sample Letter

A-1 Customer
Anywhere, U.S.A.

Dear Customer:

I wanted to advise you that our agency will no longer be representing ABC Manufacturing Company. In the course of the transition to the new sales staff, I would like for you to feel free to contact me if you have any questions or if there is anything which I can do for you to make the transition run more smoothly. Although our agency will no longer be representing ABC Manufacturing Company, I wanted to remind you that we also represent DEF, GHI and JKL Manufacturing Companies. The products they sell are generally described as follows...

I will be calling on you shortly to see if there is anything else we can do for you.

Very truly yours,

Expert Salesperson

Be Positive!

It is important to keep in mind what made you a good salesperson in the first place. Successful selling is based upon accentuating the positive and avoiding the negative. *Do not badmouth your prior employer or principal!* No customer wants to hear you say bad things about your prior principal or employer. It makes you sound like a traitor. Further, it is not good selling. You did not become successful by badmouthing your competition. You became successful by promoting the positive points about the products you are selling. You must not change that which made you successful merely because you have been terminated.

Another good example of what not to do was related to me by one of my clients several years ago. He had just recently been terminated and then went to have a meeting with his buyer to commiserate. The salesperson was relating the story of his termination to the buyer and the fact that he was not going to be paid his commissions. In essence, he was crying on the buyer's shoulder. The buyer had an easy solution. "We'll fix that principal" he said. "We'll place the business with another vendor. That'll teach them a lesson for terminating you."

This was the worst possible result for the salesperson. Not only had he just been terminated, but he also just lost any commission claim he had because the principal lost the business. If the principal is not making any sales, you will not have much of a claim to pursue in court.

You want the mental impressions and associations which your customer has with you to be positive rather than negative. If you complain about your predicament or appear depressed, then you will carry a dark cloud with you. Your customers will then want to avoid you because it is human nature to avoid negativity. People are attracted to others with positive vibrations. You always want the association in your customers' minds about you to be positive rather than negative.

Competing with Your Ex-Employer/Ex-Principal: The Tail Wagging the Dog Scenario

One question I am frequently asked by my clients is, "Should I go after my ex-principal/ex-employer's business? That is, can I attempt to have the business transferred to my new principal or employer?"

Obviously, the first consideration is whether by doing so you would be violating any restrictive covenant or agreement not to compete with your prior employer/principal (see Chapter Two). As indicated previously, you must presume that these agreements are enforceable.

Even if there is no agreement not to compete, you must also be sure not to use any confidential or proprietary information belonging to your prior employer or principal. Even if there is no written agreement prohibiting the use of confidential information, in most jurisdictions there is a common law or statutory prohibition against using your prior employer's confidential or proprietary information against them. Again, be cautious not to violate any such written agreement, or common law, or statutory duty. You should discuss this issue with a lawyer before taking any action. In many industries, however, there is very little confidential or proprietary information. In many cases, prices are well-known and may even be published.

Assuming there is no contractual, common law, or statutory prohibition, my advice to my clients is to try to get whatever business they can. Obviously, if there was any loyalty on behalf of your prior employer or principal, they would not have terminated you in the first place. Loyalty is no longer an issue.

Clients will often ask me, "How will attempting to move the business affect my lawsuit?" My answer is that it will necessarily reduce the potential recovery in your lawsuit if you are able to replace all of the business with your new principal. Such a question, however, demonstrates that the client's priorities are somewhat skewed. The tail is wagging the dog.

I tell my clients that their principal responsibility is to maximize the dollars generated in their business, not necessarily to have the best possible lawsuit. In some cases, maximizing dollars is done by pursuing a lawsuit for the unpaid commissions. In other cases, it may be by attempting to have the business re-sourced to your new employer or principal. The fact that having the business re-sourced may damage your lawsuit should not be the principal consideration of a salesperson. The issue is what action will generate the most dollars in the salesperson's pocket, not what will be best for the lawsuit.

I typically handle my cases on a one-third contingent fee basis. I tell my clients that I will be receiving one-third of any money I recover for them through their lawsuit. If my clients are able to re-source their business and get paid in that manner, as far as I am concerned, more power to them. I have no problem with that. As I indicated earlier in this book, my objective is for my clients to be winners. If being a winner means obtaining recovery outside of the legal system, then I try to encourage this.

Generally, it is not easy to re-source business to a new principal, and it may take years to do this. The sooner, however, that the salesperson begins working on this, the more likely they will reap the benefits at some point in time. You must remember that this can create credibility problems. It is hard to make the transition from telling your customer that principal A is the best, to now asserting that principal B is the best.

Generating dollars through litigation is not a very efficient way for a business to obtain revenue. Aside from the attorney fees, many claims are compromised. I encourage my clients to seek to have the business moved to their new principal/employer any time they are able to do so.

Checks with Restrictive Language

In the termination stage of your relationship, principals or employers will often attempt to buy out of commission liability by sending a check with language either on the front or back of the check which purports to release the principal from any further liability. *As a general rule, do not cash checks with restrictive language!*

Thomas Delegeorge v T.E. Fiddler & Associates

Over ten years ago I represented a salesperson by the name of Thomas Delegeorge who had an agreement with a sales representative agency. The deal was that he was supposed to be paid a commission on any business which the agency did with a principal by whom Delegeorge was previously employed.

In Delegeorge's "view", the sales agency did not comply with the agreement. Ultimately, Delegeorge resigned from his employment with the agency. Upon his termination, he received two checks. One was for reimbursement of his expenses for travel, entertainment, and automobile. The other was for his salary to the effective termination date, plus approximately ten days of additional pay. Both checks contained language on the reverse side stating that the cashing of the check constituted a full and complete release of any claims against the agency. Accompanying the check was a letter confirming that Delegeorge would introduce his replacement to the customers, even after the effective termination date.

Delegeorge crossed off the restrictive language of the checks and attempted to negotiate them. They were first returned unpaid because of the deletion. The checks were reissued with the same language. Delegeorge again crossed off the language and deposited the checks. The second time the checks were paid.

My office later filed suit for the unpaid commissions and the defendant filed a Motion for Summary Judgment,[30] arguing that by cashing the checks, Delegeorge had released his employer from any further commission obligations. My argument in response was that there was no consideration[31] for the release, and the checks merely compensated Delegeorge for the money which was indisputably owed. Part of the problem, however, was that he was paid approximately ten days' worth of salary subsequent to his termination date. My explanation for that was that the additional pay was to purchase Mr. Delegeorge's service as an independent contractor subsequent to termination to introduce the new salesperson to the customers, which in fact he did.

---

[30] A Motion for Summary Judgment or Summary Disposition by a principal is generally a request that the judge dismiss the case due to legal deficiencies.

[31] "Consideration" has been defined as "some right, interest, profit or benefit accruing to one party, or some forbearance, detriment, loss, or responsibility, given, suffered or undertaken by the other." Consideration is an essential element of a contract. Restatement, 2d, Contracts § 17(1), 71.

Unfortunately, the trial court agreed with the defendants and granted defendant's motion for summary judgment. I was convinced that our legal position was sound and we appealed the matter to the Michigan Court of Appeals. We ultimately were successful and the decision of the trial court was overturned. Unfortunately, our case languished in the Court of Appeals for four years. After the case was remanded to the trial court, we settled the claim.

Even though we were able to get around the restrictive language on the checks in that particular case, it is generally not worth the risk. *Do not accept or cash any checks with restrictive language because it may void your claim.*

Don't Shoot Yourself in the Foot

One point I try to stress with my clients is that they should always handle themselves in an honest and ethical manner in dealing with their principal or customers. If anyone is to act dishonestly or unethically, let it be your principal or employer and not you. Aside from the fact that it is the right thing to do, honesty sells to a jury and dishonesty does not.

I could not come up with an example here without embarrassing one or more of my clients. You will just have to trust me on this one.

The *Disclosure* Lesson: Get the Job Done

A few years ago, I saw the movie *Disclosure,* based upon the book by Michael Creighton.[32] In the movie, Michael Douglas played the part of an employee suing for sexual harassment committed by the character played by Demi Moore.   Michael Douglas filed a lawsuit for sexual harassment while he was still an employee.

One of the key parts in the movie was when Michael Douglas realized that he was spending more time and energy on his lawsuit than he was in doing his job for his employer. Demi Moore was attempting to set up Michael Douglas for termination based upon allegedly poor performance. This would have given the employer the opportunity to argue that the termination was because of poor performance rather than because of filing the lawsuit for sexual harassment. Further, the employer could argue that Michael Douglas was a bad employee and the lawsuit was all sour grapes. Once Michael Douglas realized that his principal responsibility was to do the best possible job he could for his employer, he was able to demonstrate that it was Demi Moore who violated her obligation to the employer rather than he. He was able to resolve the lawsuit in a positive manner and did not give the employer an opportunity to terminate him for poor performance.

This is a valuable lesson for any salesperson who is in the termination stage of his agreement. You must remember that your principal obligation as an employee is to do the

---

[32] Alfred A. Knopp, Inc., N.Y. 1994.

best possible job you can for your employer, regardless of whether you may file or have filed a lawsuit. You must not give your employer an opportunity to create a record to terminate you for poor performance. Any time there is any commission dispute, whether it has gotten to the point of litigation or not, you must work doubly hard to do the best possible job you can. This is often difficult because it is hard to be motivated to work for an employer who is not paying you what you have earned or who is in the process of attempting to fire you. You must remain vigilant and work even harder under these circumstances. Never give your employer ammunition to prove at trial that you were not doing your job. That can significantly damage your claim.

7

Litigating Your Commission Dispute

To Sue or Not to Sue

We have come to the point at which, either before or after termination, you know that you are going to have to fight to get paid your commissions. You essentially have three choices at this point: (1) hire an attorney and file a lawsuit to negotiate a resolution of your claim;[33] (2) attempt to negotiate a resolution of the claim on your own; or (3) do nothing.

Whatever choice you make is dependent upon several factors, many of which are very personal. Obviously a key consideration is the economics of the situation. Lawsuits can be expensive, and a key consideration is the amount of commissions in dispute. There will have to be a determination made as to whether the claim is economically justifiable. If you discuss this matter with an attorney, be sure to get an estimate of the total fees

---

[33] For strategic reasons, I ordinarily prefer to file a lawsuit first and then negotiate later.

and expenses involved. There are no hard and fast rules regarding at what point your claim becomes economically justifiable.

Regardless of the economics, there can be a substantial amount of stress involved in litigating any type of claim. Sometimes this stress is very subtle, other times it is not. Some people handle depositions and the other myriad aspects of a lawsuit more easily than others. Some clients seem to enjoy the battle and others can not handle the conflict. I have had some clients for whom the avoidance of the stress was more important to them than a fair resolution of their claim. In some cases, we have settled claims for significantly less than they were worth because my clients were more interested in avoiding the stress and the conflict than maximizing their recovery. This is a very personal issue and varies from client to client.

The decision to settle a case is always that of my client. I view it as my responsibility to give my client my evaluation of the strengths and weaknesses of the claim. The ultimate decision to accept any settlement or go to trial rests with my client.

There is one client of mine, named Jerry Gitre, whom I represented in a couple of matters. He is very persistent and refuses to accept what he considers to be an injustice by a principal. One of Jerry's cases resulted in a Michigan Supreme Court decision in 1972, entitled *Gitre v. Kessler Products Co., Inc.*, 198 NW2d 405 (Mich. 1972). In that particular case, Jerry's principal, Kessler Products, unilaterally classified one of Jerry's largest accounts as a "house account" and discontinued the payment of commissions on the account. Later, two more large accounts were likewise reclassified.

Jerry successfully appealed an adverse trial court decision first through the Michigan Court of Appeals and later to the Michigan Supreme Court. The Supreme Court, in a decision written by Chief Justice T.M. Cavanaugh, reversed the lower court's decision and remanded the matter for trial. Jerry Gitre had a successful trial result in that case.

I handled a jury trial in another matter for Jerry Gitre in December of 1995. In that particular case, Jerry had been terminated by Freedland Industries Corporation, and we were litigating Jerry's right to commissions after termination. The jury awarded us every penny of the commissions we sought, approximately $250,000, plus interest as well as additional damages of $100,000, under the Michigan Sales Commission Act, and attorney fees.[34]

Jerry made a comment to me one time that I feel is quite significant. He told me that he gets upset with salespeople who have a commission claim and choose not to pursue it. Jerry's argument is that the terminated salesperson owes it to all other salespersons to pursue his

---

[34] Frankly, it helped in this case that the only witnesses who testified for Freedland were lawyers. One of the principal owners was a lawyer, who actually was a good friend of Jerry Gitre. One of the key managers was also a lawyer who had been in private practice for several years before being hired by his ex-client. It is my personal opinion that one of the best ways to screw up a business is to hire a lawyer to run it.

claim. Otherwise, if a principal or employer is able to avoid payment of commissions which are owed because the salesperson chose not to pursue it, this only encourages the principal or employer to do it again to another salesperson. Jerry's argument was that salespeople need to stand up for their own rights, and also for the rights of other salespeople. Frankly, I believe there is much truth to that.

One of the reasons why employers and principals terminate salespeople is because it is profitable for them to do so. If it becomes unprofitable, it should occur less frequently.

The reality of the situation is that if a company has ten commissioned salespeople whom it chooses to terminate without paying the commissions which are rightfully earned, there may be one, two, or three of them who choose not to take any action. Of the remaining, perhaps two or three may hire an attorney who is not skilled enough in sales commission disputes to obtain an appropriate recovery. Of the remaining few, maybe one or two may accept a significant compromise for one reason or another. Out of the ten, the principal may only have to pay full value on one or two claims. Accordingly, the principal can still make money on the average.

Be Prepared for the Long Haul

As indicated in Chapter Two, it is difficult to resolve a claim in less than one year. Part of the reason for this is that in my practice, as indicated previously, we like to go back and audit commissions for two to three years prior to termination. Often we engage in significant discovery battles attempting to obtain the sales records in order to accurately determine whether pre-termination commissions have been properly paid. Many principals or employers make it difficult to obtain post-termination sales information in order to adequately calculate commissions. Discovery battles can last for several months. Further, in order to evaluate a claim adequately, generally at least two or three depositions are required. By the time all of this takes place, twelve months can easily pass.

You must be prepared for the long haul in litigating a commission dispute. You must also keep in mind that many principals use time to their advantage in an attempt to place economic pressure on the terminated salesperson. In some cases this can be very effective. This is one reason why, as suggested in Chapter Two, it is important that you put money away to prepare for the possibility of litigating a commission claim. It will help to put you in a stronger position if and when termination ever occurs. If the termination does not occur, you will generally be able to find a use for the money which you have saved.

Don't Allow Yourself to Be Treated Like a Mushroom

Unfortunately, some lawyers have a tendency to treat their clients like mushrooms, i.e., the clients are kept in the dark and fed horse manure. Typically, I find that this happens when the attorneys are inexperienced and are afraid that their clients will find out.

You must treat your lawsuit like any other business matter. Most successful salespersons or business people in general have become successful because they leave very few matters to chance. Being a plaintiff in a lawsuit is no different. If you do not understand or are not aware of what is happening, you must assume that nothing is being done. This is not to say that the client is to be the captain of the ship; this role should belong to the lawyer. The client, however, should at all times be well informed and aware as to the status and progress of the lawsuit at any given time. If you are uncertain, *ask*!

In my practice, I consider my clients to be my partners and generally the feeling is mutual. I will never know as much about my clients' business as they do. My clients will never know as much about litigating commission disputes as I do. It is by working as a team that we can generally be the most successful.

Fortunately, in my business I have a tendency to deal with very successful, intelligent business people. Generally this makes my job easier.

I make it a practice to copy my clients on all communications and all pleadings. I also encourage my clients to read and understand all of the documents and pleadings which are filed. It is vitally important for a salesperson in a commission dispute to understand fully the legal and factual basis for their claim. Otherwise, depositions can be quite damaging. I cannot overemphasize the importance of understanding the basic legal concepts in sales commission disputes. This is true regardless of whether or not you have an active commission claim. If you are going to be in the sales business for the long run, you owe it to yourself to understand the basic legal principles involved in sales law. This is one of the key reasons why I have written my articles and this book. Part of my goal is to educate salespeople as to the extent of their rights so that they can protect themselves adequately when the circumstances and needs arise.

Knowledge is power. If you know more than your opponent, generally good things will happen.

Get an Expert, or "The Secret to Life Is One Thing"

Often, it costs no more to get an expert than a novice. Most contingent fee arrangements are approximately the same. In fact, many attorneys charge more than one-third. Frankly, it is generally legal to charge more than one-third in commercial litigation. I ordinarily, however, restrict my fees to one-third. My clients have to work too hard for their commissions to pay much more than that in attorney fees.

Another problem and criticism which I sometimes have of attorneys in general is that often they believe that since they have a law degree, they can handle any type of legal problem. Partially this is a function of there being too many lawyers. It is sometimes difficult for a lawyer to admit to a client that he is not the proper person to handle a particular claim, especially a big claim with a potentially large fee. Frankly, this is a very fertile area for attorney malpractice. You would not go to a general practitioner for heart surgery. Similarly, be wary of using a general practitioner for a specialized legal problem.

Be sure to ask the attorney whether he has handled similar types of claims in the past. Additionally, don't be afraid to ask for client references relating to similar claims. If you receive a reference, contact the client to find out whether he was satisfied. It is important to me when a case is over that my client is satisfied. I will generally try to go above and beyond the call of duty to ensure that. Partially, this is for selfish reasons, because most of my business comes from referrals from satisfied clients. This may also be because of my background. I was an account executive for a vendor for General Motors when I was in law school. My emphasis was on customer satisfaction. In my opinion, attorneys should be more interested in making sure that their clients are satisfied than in maximizing legal fees.

One of the principles which I try to follow in my professional and personal life was most succinctly stated by the great philosopher Curly, played by Jack Palance in the movie *City Slickers*. Curly said to the character played by Billy Crystal, "The secret to life is one thing." Billy Crystal spent the entire movie trying to figure out what that one thing was. Was it money? Was it love? Was it happiness? Was it success? What was the one thing?

By the end of the movie, Billy Crystal's character realized that the "one thing" was different for everyone. Curly's one thing was different from Billy Crystal's character's one thing. The secret is to find out what your one thing is and then try to focus on that. As it relates to my law practice, I focus on representing salespeople: manufacturer's representatives and other commissioned salespersons. I believe I am the best lawyer in the world in my area of expertise. I do not believe that I am the smartest lawyer in the world, but I have analyzed and solved more sales commission related problems in the past twenty years than all but perhaps a very few people. It doesn't take magic or genius, just a willingness to expend the effort and the discipline to accept only a high level of personal performance. It is no different than what any salesperson does. It makes no difference what you sell. Try to be the best at what you do.

Curly's principle also teaches you to be realistic. By striving to be the best sales commission lawyer, I necessarily have to accept the reality that I cannot be the best in everything I do. I have to accept my golf handicap, which happens to be a five at this time, and realize that I do not have the time nor commitment to be a scratch golfer. I am not willing to make the necessary sacrifices at this time in my life. Golf is one of my avocations, not my vocation.

If you are able to, try to find a lawyer with the experience as well as the time and the inclination to properly focus his energy and attention on your problem.

Contingent or Hourly?

Most of the time when you contact an attorney, you have the option to hire the attorney on a contingent fee (a percentage of the recovery) or an hourly rate. I almost never handle commission disputes on an hourly fee basis. Part of the reason for this is that I handle my practice the way most salespeople do. I gear my practice toward obtaining the maximum recovery in the least amount of time practicable. My objective is to accomplish a specific result, namely, winning the case. I do not want my motivation to be based upon creating busywork or lengthening the time to resolve the claim so that I make more money. I want my mind set to be winning rather than generating hourly fees.

A recent lawsuit I handled is an example. The names of the client and the law firm will remain anonymous because I do not want to embarrass the lawyers involved. In this particular case, we submitted a settlement demand relatively early in the case in the low 6 figures. Our proposal was rejected with indignation. The defense attorneys scheduled multiple depositions and, in fact, took several days worth of video deposition from my client. Perhaps they thought they could intimidate him.[35] Ultimately, the case mediated for approximately $25,000 more than our initial settlement proposal. My client accepted the mediation amount.

---

[35] My typical reaction to this is "Methinks thou dost protest too much."

In Michigan, mediation, which is now referred to as case evaluation, is nonbinding and both parties have the opportunity to accept or reject the mediation evaluation. If both parties accept, the case settles. If either party rejects and the case proceeds to trial, the objecting party must better the mediation award by more than ten percent, or be liable to pay the other party's costs and attorney fees incurred as a result of the rejection of the mediation award. The defendant in this case rejected the mediation award. On the eve of trial, we ended up negotiating a settlement for approximately 3 times the amount of our initial settlement demand and more than 2 ½ times the amount of the mediation award. My client was very satisfied, but I often wonder how satisfied the defendant was. Frankly, in my opinion, the defense attorneys did not do a great service for their client. Between the cost of the settlement and attorney fees, the defendant paid more than three times the amount it would have cost to settle the case in the early stages.

Litigation Is War

You must keep in mind that when you are involved in a lawsuit for hundreds of thousands, or even more than a million dollars, this is the legal equivalent of war. You must expect the opposition to use against you every legal weapon which they have in their arsenal. Don't assume that because you are legally correct or that you have a contract which obligates the defendant to make the payment it will be any different.[36]

---

[36] Please refer to my discussion regarding *Tech Interface v Andrew Corporation, supra* on pages 114-117.

A few years ago I was involved in a case entitled *Don R. Bowerman, Inc., v Manufacturers Products Co.* (MPC). Manufacturers Products had undergone a change in ownership and sought to re-negotiate my client's sales representation agreement. The original agreement, which was due to expire in a few months, provided that in the event of termination or expiration, my client was entitled to receive commissions for approximately three years after termination or expiration. The total commission exposure was approximately $2,000,000. The proposal for a new contract from Manufacturers Products entailed a new agreement which would, in essence, have paid the $2,000,000 to my client over the course of three years. The difference was that he would have been required to continue to work during the three-year period, while under the existing contract he would not. After the expiration of the three years, the commission entitlement would be extinguished.

It made no sense to accept the proposal by MPC when, if nothing else was done, my client would receive the same three years' worth of commissions without any additional work, and could find another job or another principal to represent as long as it was not with a competitor. When it was evident my client would not compromise his claim, MPC filed a demand for arbitration. The claim was filed with the American Arbitration Association, even though the arbitration provision of the contract did not provide for arbitration through this organization. Under the contract, each party had the opportunity to select their own arbitrator, and the two so selected would select a neutral. If the arbitrators selected by the parties could not agree upon a neutral, the American Arbitration Association would pick the neutral.

Our office immediately filed suit to enforce arbitration under the terms of the contract. I wanted to pick my own arbitrator rather than have the American Arbitration Association pick the arbitrators. The judge agreed and enforced arbitration in accordance with the agreement.

Frankly, I believe that MPC was hopeful that the arbitrators would somehow compromise the claim which frequently occurs in arbitration. I also believe we were able to minimize this possibility by having some control over the selection of the arbitrators.

The only real issue the defendant in this case had with my client was that my client was paid a small commission from a tooling source which the defendant contended was a violation of the agreement. MPC made metal stampings. These are typically manufactured by compressing or stamping steel into molds or dies. The metal dies are sometimes referred to as "tools." In some cases, manufacturer's representatives get paid a commission for tooling or dies, but generally they do not. Oridinarily, the major automotive companies own the tooling and purchase it at cost from the stamping companies. The stamping companies are supposed to earn a profit on the production parts, but generally not on the tooling.

In this particular case, however, we had a signed agreement from the president and prior owner agreeing that my client could be paid a commission from the tooling source in order to help fund the hiring of an additional employee. The commission, in any event, was approximately $2,000. In my opinion, the payment of the small commission provided no justification for MPC's attempt to avoid the payment of approximately $2 million in termination commissions.

Our arbitration panel consisted of two highly experienced litigation attorneys and a retired trial judge. The plaintiff arbitrator was a friend of mine who had successfully handled large commission disputes.[37] The defense arbitrator was from one of the largest defense firms in Michigan, an attorney whom I knew would be a formidable advocate for MPC. The retired trial judge was an excellent trial judge who is as honest as the day is long.

The arbitrators accepted my client's position and ordered the defendant to pay 100% of the termination commissions. The principle concession made to the defendant was a failure to award the penalties under the Michigan Sales Representative Commission Act of an additional $100,000. There were also some disputes regarding deductions taken during the course of the relationship. The arbitrators refused to award us the disputed pre-termination commissions. We were very satisfied with the results. My client, however, went for more than one year without any income. Fortunately, he

---

[37] Under the rules of the American Arbitration Association, the arbitrator was considered a "party appointed arbitrator" and was entitled to be inclined toward my client's position.

was able to weather the twelve-month period because of his investments.[38]

Frankly, I believe the defendant in this case had no real defense against the commission claim under the contract. In my opinion, the defendant merely attempted to use the withholding of the commissions as a weapon to force a compromise. Fortunately, my client was in a position to refuse to compromise and received 100% of his post-termination claim. The defendant's strategy in this case would have worked in many other instances with other clients who did not have the financial resources to go without any income for one year. Often there is substantial pressure to compromise the claim when the plaintiff's money starts to run out. This is a fact of life in the litigation business.

Shoot First, Ask Questions Later

Frequently, sales commission disputes are easier to negotiate to resolution than other types of litigation. One reason is that most manufacturing companies are not in the litigation business like insurance companies are. There is a significant difference between sales commission disputes and personal injury litigation.

---

[38] Interestingly, we had to have another arbitration hearing approximately four years after the initial hearing to address underpayments during a two year post-termination period. We recovered an additional approximately $130,000. This is another example of the importance of verifying the accuracy of your commission checks.

For example, if a person were injured in an automobile accident and suffered a broken leg, the claim would typically be handled by an insurance company. Insurance companies have adjusters whose job it is to handle legal claims. The adjusters have relationships with defense attorneys with whom they socialize. Often the defense attorneys take the adjusters out to play golf, to the theater, and the like. If not for the personal injury lawsuit, the insurance adjuster and the defense attorneys would have nothing to do.

Additionally, there are computer data banks containing information such as types of injuries, county where the lawsuit is pending, prior claims by the injured person, and other factors which are used to evaluate these claims. If a plaintiff attorney makes a demand for ten times more than the value of a broken leg as determined by the adjuster, the defense attorney's evaluation, and the computer analysis, the insurance company is more than willing to take the matter to trial. This protects the job of the adjuster and provides business for his friends in the defense attorney's office. There often is no real incentive to resolve the claim. This is especially true in medical malpractice cases in which many insurance companies have a policy of litigating all but the worst cases. The insurance company is in the business of litigating claims.

The circumstances are substantially different in a sales commission dispute. In many cases, this may be the first lawsuit the manufacturing company has ever had. Manufacturing companies are not in the business of litigating these claims. Their business is manufacturing parts or other products and selling them to their customers. Additionally, unlike the insurance company, the exposure faced by the manufacturing company can be significantly higher than the commissions which are in dispute.

Any time a salesperson is terminated, there can be stress in the relationship between the principal and its customer. Often the salesperson had a good relationship with the buyers involved and the buyers may be sympathetic to the salesperson. Generally, it was the salesperson who was doing the socializing with the buyers and otherwise establishing the rapport and personal working relationship. When you take the stress created by a change in sales representation and add to that the typical stress in a relationship because of normal quality and delivery problems, the relationship between the manufacturer and the customer can become tenuous. When you add to the mix the possibility that the customer's buyers and managers may be subpoenaed to testify in a deposition or in court, this creates additional pressure. Typically, buyers and managers have more than enough work to do and they are not happy to have time taken away from their business to participate in court proceedings involving third parties.

The combination of all of these factors can sometimes put the business at risk. In some circumstances, the customer may have indicated to the manufacturer that if they are not able to resolve their problems with their salespeople, they will find a manufacturer who can. This means that the principal can be at risk not only for the commissions which are in dispute, but potentially for the loss of the business. Rather than a commission dispute of approximately $200,000, for example, the principal may now be at risk for losing $10,000,000 in annual sales. This is one of the factors which make commission disputes easier to resolve than other types of litigation.

In one recent case I handled, a local sales representative agency was earning more than $1,000,000 a year in commissions. The manufacturer, located outside of Michigan, decided that he was going to terminate the relationship and establish an in-house sales force. The manufacturer made it clear to my client that he wanted to attempt to negotiate a resolution. I stressed to my client the importance of initiating a lawsuit to attempt to ensure that the litigation would be handled in Michigan. I advised him that we would still be able to attempt to negotiate a resolution, but we would be in a much better negotiating position after the lawsuit had been filed.

After the defendant got over the initial shock of the lawsuit, the parties were able to begin their settlement discussions. Both parties made it clear that they wanted to negotiate directly without lawyers being involved.

I indicated to my client that it was important for him to have a thorough understanding of his legal position if he were going to attempt to negotiate a resolution of his claim. I provided him with all of the articles I had written, including an article entitled *The History of the Procuring Cause Doctrine in Michigan*.[39] This was a Law Review article I wrote summarizing all of the case law in Michigan dealing with the Procuring Cause Doctrine.

---

[39] Please see Gillary, *The History of the Procuring Cause Doctrine In Michigan*, 74 Mich. B.J. 1264 (1995).

We spent a substantial amount of time preparing my client for the negotiations. In part, I believe, because my client was substantially more well versed in his legal position, he was able to negotiate a resolution worth over $3,000,000. The initial proposal by the defendant was approximately $600,000. The ultimate resolution included jobs with the defendant for several members of my client's sales agency. I do not believe my client would have been able to obtain such a result if we had not filed first and if he had not spent the time to learn the appropriate legal principles.

Preparing for Depositions

There are many different ways to prepare for a deposition if you are the plaintiff in a sales commission dispute. Some attorneys spend hours with their clients, bombarding them with every possible question they think the opposing attorney may ask. I have a tendency not to do this. I feel the best way for a salesperson to prepare for a deposition is to familiarize himself or herself thoroughly with the keys facts in the case. This should involve reviewing all correspondence, all pleadings, all discovery responses, and all relevant file material. We then review key areas I expect the other attorney to inquire into, but we do not generally rehearse specific answers to specific questions.

The problem with preparing for specific questions is that if the attorney does not ask the specific question for which you prepared, the witness now has to think rather than to parrot. This can create anxiety and apprehension which gives the appearance that the witness is not being truthful. I prefer to attempt to familiarize my client with the specific topics which will be covered, paying particular attention to the agreement between the parties. My goal is to prepare the client to respond to the questions rather than to have prearranged answers.

When I take a deposition of a defendant, I do not have a list of questions I intend to ask. I may have a one-page outline, but the deposition is very free-flowing. The answer the witness gives generally dictates what the next question will be. It is virtually impossible to anticipate every question an attorney will ask. You are generally much better off to follow a few general rules:

1. Be adequately prepared and remember it is almost impossible to be overprepared.

2. Tell the truth.

3. Don't try to anticipate what the attorney will ask you. This takes mental energy away from formulating a direct answer to the question.

4. Get a good night's sleep the night before.

Included below are some additional suggestions I provide to my clients to help them prepare.

General Rules

1. In general, you should answer each question directly. Try to answer yes or no if possible. Each answer should be short and concise with a minimum of explanation.

2. Do not guess or speculate. If you do not know the answer to a question, or you do not recall, a fair answer is, "I don't know" or "I don't recall." Do not attempt to testify about why someone else may have done something or about any thought processes which may have been going on in another's mind.

3. Do not attempt to educate the other attorney if he does not understand the business. Many attorneys defending commission cases are not familiar with the sales business. Unfortunately, many salespeople have a tendency to want to be very helpful and provide explanations. If the opposing attorney is having difficulty, that is his problem. Don't help him!

4. You must remember that the purpose of the deposition from the defendant's standpoint is to obtain as much information as possible, which he may use against you. Although there are exceptions, generally what you do not say cannot be used against you.

5. In general, you should not attempt to give percentages of time or hours, weekly or monthly,

spent on a given principal or employer's business. Unless you keep specific and accurate time records, you should avoid any quantification in answering any of these questions. Typically, you spend as much time as is necessary on any particular project. At one point in the process you may be spending a high percentage of your time and at another point a low percentage. Generally your answer should be to the effect that you spend as much time as is necessary to accomplish the specific task. Defense attorneys will attempt to compare the dollars you are seeking to the actual amount of time spent in order to come up with what may appear to be an unreasonable hourly rate. This is why the quantification should be avoided when possible.

6. Try to avoid using the terminology "servicing an account." A manufacturer's representative does not generally get paid to "service an account." Manufacturer's representatives are paid to *sell*. You only get paid if a sale is made. The reason it is important to avoid this terminology is that an attorney for a principal will attempt to get you to quantify what portion of the commission is to compensate you for "selling" and what portion of the commission is to compensate you for "servicing." The logical progression of this is that since you no longer will be servicing an account after termination, the portion of the commission is intended to pay you for "servicing" should be deducted from the commission you are claiming. We always take the position that the commission

is to compensate you for the selling activity which is done and sometimes the years which are spent to procure the business in advance of the issuance of the purchase order. The commissions paid after production has commenced, and even during the post-termination period, are to compensate you not for servicing the account, but for the initial sales activity. Additionally, the work you will be doing after the purchase order has been issued is geared toward either maximizing the sales on the existing purchase order or toward obtaining the next purchase order. *Everything is selling: there is no servicing.*

7. Never acknowledge that your employer or principal can change your compensation plan or your commission rate at their discretion. If you agree that your principal or employer can change your compensation plan or commission rate at any time, you are agreeing that they can eliminate commissions at any time without your consent. You should never acknowledge this. First of all, it's generally not true. Your employer or principal generally cannot retroactively alter your compensation plan. They can make changes prospectively but generally not retroactively. Secondly, commission plans and compensation plans are a matter of contract. There may be an implied threat that if you do not agree you will be terminated, but you still have the right to either agree or disagree. Never acknowledge that the power and ability to make these changes rests exclusively with your employer or principal.

Typical Topics You Can Expect to Be Covered

1. **Educational background**. Be prepared to discuss in detail your educational background. Further, assume that the defense attorney will already have done a background information check to verify any information in any resumes or employment applications, including the receipt of any degrees mentioned. Never misrepresent your credentials in any employment application. In some cases this can be used to defeat a wrongful termination claim.

2. **Employment background**. This is generally used to establish your expertise or lack thereof in a particular field.

3. **Other principals represented**. You can expect to be questioned regarding other principals you represent. In general, you are required to answer these types of questions. An exception is when the identity of principals or customers is confidential and proprietary and can be used against you or your principal in the marketplace. It is also possible that the defendant may subpoena records from your other principals including copies of contracts. Generally the contractual information is discoverable.

4. **History of contact and relationship with defendant**. Expect to be extensively questioned concerning how your relationship started and any

significant events which occurred during the course of the relationship.

5. **Agreement with principal**. This is generally the single most significant area of questioning. The agreement with your principal contains the foundation for any claim.

   a) Written or oral

      i.   If the contract is in writing, be sure that you have a thorough understanding of all of the key provisions. Especially concentrate on the provisions regarding compensation and termination.

      ii. If the agreement is oral, be prepared to justify the contractual basis for your claim based upon the oral agreement.

      iii. The contractual basis for the claim must be reviewed extensively with your counsel to ensure that you have an adequate understanding of your legal position.

b) Account-procured agreement or order-procured agreement—which is it? Are you being compensated for sales made to accounts which you procure or only on the basis of orders which you have procured?

c) You must be fully aware of which orders or accounts you are seeking sales commissions for as well as the names of the buyers. Review the names of the key buyers. It is hard to convince someone you procured the business if you can't remember who the buyer was.

6. **Claims raised in complaint.** You must assume you will be questioned extensively regarding the specific claims which have been raised in the complaint. Review the complaint and understand the substance of the allegations and the foundation for your claim.

7. **Discovery responses/affidavits.** Review any previously signed discovery responses or affidavits. Any variation in your testimony from what you have previously signed can significantly damage your credibility.

8. **Claims raised in counterclaim.** Review any counterclaim and be sure that you understand the basis for any such claim being made against you.

9. **Pertinent correspondence.** Review all pertinent correspondence with your principal which affects

any issue such as the agreement, termination, compensation, performance, customer satisfaction or dissatisfaction, etc. Assume you will be questioned extensively on any relevant correspondence.

10. **Key meetings.** Expect to be questioned extensively concerning any key meetings with your principal. This would include the meeting in which the original agreement was made if there is an oral contract, as well as any discussions concerning interpretation or anyone's understanding of the agreement if there was a written contract. Additionally, the termination meeting is very significant. You should review all of these meetings in detail with your attorney.

The best way to prepare for deposition is to be sure that you have reviewed the factual matters sufficiently to refresh your recollection of what has transpired. You should be better prepared than the other attorney concerning the factual documentation. It is important that you prepare in this manner because it is impossible to anticipate all of the potential questions which may be asked by the other attorney. If too much time is spent on trying to formulate answers to specific questions, the tendency is to try to provide a specific answer regardless of whether it is responsive to the question. This can affect your credibility and can be confusing to you, which can do more harm than good. Just listen to the question and give a short, concise, direct answer.

A good deposition can make your case, just as well as a bad deposition can substantially damage it.

Suing While Still Employed

There are certain circumstances under which it is advisable to commence a lawsuit with either a principal or employer while a salesperson is still employed. A case in which I have recently been involved is a good example.

We have settled the case and have entered into a confidentiality agreement. Accordingly, I will use no names.

I was first contacted by Salesperson A, who was employed by a manufacturing company.[40] The employer had recently been purchased by another company, and it was made clear to the salespeople that the commission plan was going to be eliminated. Ultimately, I had a meeting with some of the salespeople who stood to lose approximately $1,000,000 each in commissions. Each of the employees had an agreement which laid out the commission arrangement and contained no provision limiting commissions in the event of a termination. Within approximately the next two weeks, the company was going to unilaterally impose a new salary and bonus arrangement. All of the salespersons had obtained

---

[40] Incidentally, this client was referred to me by one of my other clients for whom I had successfully handled a case.

significant automotive production business which would be generating commissions for five or more years. Although my clients wanted to be paid their commissions, they also wanted to retain their jobs if possible. These are normally mutually exclusive options.

A decision was made to file suit prior to the effective date of the new plan so that there could be no argument made that the salespersons had accepted the terms of a new compensation package (see Chapter One). The filing of the lawsuit clearly sent a message to the employer that the salespersons were not in agreement with the unilaterally modified commission plan.

Needless to say, it got somewhat exciting for my clients after the company was served with the summons, complaint, discovery requests, and deposition notices. We made it clear to the employer's attorneys that we were still willing to negotiate. I felt that if the employer was able to get past the initial knee-jerk reaction of terminating my clients, it would recognize that it was in its best interest to negotiate a resolution to retain my clients and to pay them their commissions. Frankly, the employer was in somewhat of a Catch-22 position. If the employer terminated my clients, the employer's key contact people with the customers would be gone. My clients had procured over 60% of the total sales of approximately $60 million per year. Additionally, the employer would face exposure of additional damages of $100,000 per salesperson, plus attorney fees under the Michigan Sales Representative Commission Act. This means that the termination could cost the employer not only the commissions which may have to be paid to the salespeople, but an additional $100,000 plus per employee. Further, and more importantly, there would have been substantial damage caused due to the disruption in the relationship with the customer.

If the company did not do anything, we ultimately would have a legal determination as to the company's liability to pay commissions in accordance with the original agreement. Fortunately, we were able to negotiate a resolution in a half-day meeting in my office. The meeting consisted of myself and my clients and the sales manager of the defendant, plus attorneys and one of the key owners. My clients were very satisfied.

This demonstrates the importance of obtaining competent legal advice sooner rather than later. If the salespeople had not taken any action until after the effective date of the new compensation plan, they could have been deemed to have accepted the new arrangement. This would have weakened their position substantially. You must be willing to allow your attorney to be innovative in order to obtain the best possible results.

Sales Commission Acts

Many states now have sales commission acts which provide protection to commissioned salespeople who have been terminated and have to sue for their commissions.[41] Michigan for example, has a sales

---

[41] Currently thirty-three states have statutes protecting the rights of sales representatives to be paid their

commission act which was passed in 1992. The Michigan Sales Representative Commission Act (SRCA) mandates the payment of commissions to sales representatives who have been terminated and provides additional damages for the intentional failure to pay earned commissions. The additional damages under the Michigan SRCA can reach a maximum of $100,000, with the possibility of obtaining costs and attorney fees. Many other states have similar laws protecting commissioned salespeople. Be sure to have your attorney review and discuss with you any sales commission acts which may apply.

My office represented the plaintiff sales representative in the most significant case to date involving the Michigan SRCA. This was the case of Kenneth Henes Special Projects Procurement, Marketing and Consulting Corporation v Continental Biomass Industries, Inc.

Plaintiff is a one-man manufacturer's representative sales agency, owned by Ken Henes, that specializes in selling new and used construction, environmental, and demolition waste processing equipment. Defendant Continental Biomass Industries (CBI) is a New Hampshire corporation that manufactures large grinding machines used to process trees and wood waste into mulch. CBI's machines typically have a selling price of between $500,000 and $1.5 million. Ultimately there was a dispute between Henes and CBI regarding the payment of a sales commission on the sale of four machines. A lawsuit was filed by our office in June of 1998 seeking the

---

earned commissions. You should check with your lawyer to determine if one of these statutes is applicable to your claim.

unpaid commissions together with the penalty damages under Michigan's SRCA.

After a six day trial in June of 1999 in the courtroom of Federal District Judge Gerald Rosen, the jury awarded 100% of the commissions we were asking for in the amount of $135,193. The jury also found that there was an intentional failure to pay the commissions on three of the four transactions and therefore a violation of the SRCA. Judge Rosen added the penalty of $100,000 plus attorney fees in the amount of $69,123 for a total judgement of approximately $325,000 including interest at that time.[42] The defendant appealed the award of the penalty damages and attorney fees but not the commission award, to the Sixth Circuit Court of Appeals in Cincinnati, Ohio.[43]

---

[42] Just before the trial was to commence, Mr. Anders Ragnarsson, the owner and president of CBI, said to my client and I, "My time is worth $5,000 per day and I expect that the trial will take 3 days. I will pay you $15,000 to settle the case and no more." Although Ken Henes was willing to settle, $15,000 was not even in the same universe.

[43] Not appealing the commission award was significant because CBI was arguing that they shouldn't be liable for the penalty damages unless they "knew commissions were due and chose not to pay them." This was later expanded to the argument that CBI shouldn't be liable for the penalty damages of $100,000 if there was a "good faith dispute". The problem for CBI however, was that by not paying or appealing the commission award of $135,193, all of their reasons for contending that they were not liable for the $100,000 in penalty damages vanished. I am finishing this book in June of 2003 and they and they still have not paid the commissions which are now almost 4 years old. Even under their own theory, CBI violated the SRCA.

The Michigan SRCA is based upon the *Model Bill for Prompt Payment of Post-Termination Commissions to Sales Representatives,* by the Bureau of Wholesale Representatives. Michigan's SRCA, however, has some substantial deviations from the Model Bill. The Model Bill contains the following provision allowing a sales representative to recover treble damages when a principal fails to comply with the commission payment requirements:

> X-004 A Principal who fails to comply with the provisions of X-002 of this subtitle shall be liable to the sales representative in a civil action for:
>
> (A) All amounts due to the sales representative plus additional damages in an amount not to exceed two times the amount of commissions due the sales representative; and
>
> (B) Attorney fees reasonably incurred by the sales representative in the action, and court costs.

Unlike the Model Bill, Michigan's SRCA includes an "intentional" standard as a prerequisite for liability under the Act. Under Michigan's SRCA, if a principal *intentionally* fails to pay commissions which are due to a sales representative within 45 days of termination (or within 45 days of the date they are due if the commissions are due after termination), the principal is liable for double damages up to a maximum penalty of $100,000. In the *Henes* case, the defendant argued that we were required to show bad faith before it could be found liable to pay the double damages under the SRCA.

Essentially the defendant was arguing that if there was a good faith dispute as to whether or not the commissions were due, then the principal could not be in violation of the SRCA. Our office was arguing that as long as the failure to pay was intentional, the double damages were owed.

During the course of the appeal, Michigan lawyers wrote three Law Review articles which addressed the trial court's decision and the proper standard for awarding penalty damages under the SRCA. The first article, written by Attorney Steven Wolock and published in the Michigan Bar Journal in November of 2000, was entitled *Michigan's Sales Representative Act Revisited*. Mr. Wolock questioned Federal District Judge Rosen's refusal to define the term "intentional" to include an element of bad faith. The second Law Review article, written by attorney Matthew Leitman and published in the MSU-DCL Law Review in late 2000, was entitled *How the Federal Courts Have Distorted the Double Damages Provision of Michigan's Sales Representative Act*. In his article, Mr. Leitman strongly argued that Judge Rosen erred and that the term "intentional" should have been defined to include an element of bad faith. Mr. Leitman also criticized the results in three other Federal Court decisions which held principals liable for penalty damages under the SRCA for intentionally refusing to pay sales commissions as required by the SRCA. Three of the four cases referred to in the article were cases our office had won including the *Henes* case.

Feeling under fire in that we were having to litigate our case not only in the court system but also in the legal publications arena,[44] my associate Kevin Albus and I wrote a Law Review article entitled *Michigan's Sales Representative Act Revisited – Again – Or, Does "Intentionally" Mean "In Bad Faith"?* This article was also published in the MSU-DCL Law Review in late 2001. One of the questions raised in our article was why the Sixth Circuit Court of Appeals (a Federal Court) should decide an issue which should be certified to the Michigan Supreme Court for decision. In diversity actions, Federal Courts generally look to the highest court in the state for guidance in interpreting that state's laws.[45]

During the argument in the Court of Appeals in Cincinnati, Sixth Circuit Judge Cornelia Kennedy made a comment to me to the effect that writing a Law Review article was an interesting way to avoid the limited briefing requirements under the Federal Rules of Appellate Procedure. I responded to the effect that since other attorneys were taking potshots at my cases in legal publications, I felt compelled to respond.

---

[44] Interestingly, Mr. Leitman represented another principal we were suing for past due commissions and penalty damages under the SRCA which was also pending in the Sixth Circuit Court of Appeals at the same time as the *Henes* case. This was the case of *Terry Barr Sales, LLC v Amcast Industrial Corporation*, case numbers 01-1097 & 01-1098. The Terry Barr case also involved the issue as to whether good faith was a defense to the penalty damages under the SRCA. Proceedings in the *Terry Barr* case were put on hold pending the outcome of the *Henes* case. Everybody has an agenda.

[45] The Federal Courts have jurisdiction in legal disputes involving state law generally if the 2 parties are from different states and there is at least $75,000 in dispute.

The Sixth Circuit, apparently picking up on the point made in our Law Review article, certified the following question to the Michigan Supreme Court:

> "What standard is appropriate in evaluating the mental state required for double damages under the Michigan Sales Representative Commission Act?"

Opposing counsel and I argued the case in the Michigan Supreme Court on November 20, 2002. On April 23, 2003, the Michigan Supreme Court issued a twelve page unanimous decision answering the certified question as follows:

> "We have accepted the certification and hold that the plain language of the statute requires only that the principal purposely fail to pay a commission when due. The statute does not require evidence of bad faith before double damages as provided in the statue may be imposed."

The Court went on to state that:

> "Under the language of the statute, it appears that the only cognizable defense to a double damages claim is if the failure to pay the commission were based on inadvertence or oversight."

I was very pleased that not only did we have a complete victory in the Michigan Supreme Court but in addition the decision was unanimous. Michigan Supreme Court Justice Robert Young who authored the Opinion, even cited our Law Review article as authority.

This was a huge victory for manufacturer's representatives and other commissioned sales representatives in the State of Michigan. The *Henes* decision means that even if there is a good faith dispute as to whether commissions are owed under the SRCA in the event of a termination, if the principal loses and is found liable to pay the commissions there is then no real defense to the penalty damages.

Frankly, the justification for the relatively low threshold of liability under the SRCA is Michigan's relatively low cap on the maximum amount of penalty damages awardable. Michigan's SRCA caps penalty damages at $100,000. The quid pro quo for the low threshold is a relatively low maximum penalty award. Michigan's SRCA is rather unique in this regard. This argument is more fully expanded upon in our Law Review article, where we analyze the various sales commission acts enacted throughout the United States.

The net effect of the Michigan Supreme Court's decision in *Henes v CBI* is that it will make it more costly for principals to withhold commissions from manufacturer's representatives and other sales representatives who transact business in Michigan. For this reason, the *Henes* decision is a big victory for manufacturer's representatives in the State of Michigan.

Re-establishing Relationships after Termination

It is often difficult to put Humpty Dumpty back together again. We have however, on rare occasions been able to reverse terminations for a minimum negotiated time period. Generally this occurs when we have negotiated a reasonable post-termination commission payout. It can often be to the advantage of both you and your principal for you to continue to call on the customer as to the existing business generating the post-termination commissions. This saves additional expense for the principal, but more importantly, it can alleviate any concern you may have that the commissions will be jeopardized by the failure of the principal to adequately maintain the business in which you are no longer involved. In some cases, it is to your advantage to maintain some contact to ensure that the principal does not lose the business which is generating the commissions.

In one particular case I handled, the sales representative agreement required the payment of commissions for two years after termination. The principal in that case indicated that he would only pay the commissions if my client continued to "service" the work. I objected, because, since my client was terminated, he was no longer required to perform any services of any kind for the principal.

Ultimately my client came to me and said that he was very concerned about the principal's ability to maintain the business if my client were no longer involved. The buyers involved got along much better with my client than they did with the principal. Ultimately we agreed that my client would continue to call on the buyers and handle any other problems related solely to the business he was being paid a commission on. Frankly, this took little time and allowed my client to be involved and to protect his substantial financial interest by maintaining the business.

Continuing to have the sales representative involved in maintaining contact with the customers on existing business which he is being paid on, even after termination, can result in a win/win situation for both the principal and the sales representative. It eliminates the need for the principal to hire an additional person to handle the day-to-day contact on that business. It benefits the sales representative because he is able to protect his commission. You should keep this in mind as a way to amicably resolve some commission problems.

EPILOGUE

My purpose in writing this book has been to help salespeople to think about the problems which they are likely to encounter throughout their sales careers and to have a plan to deal with those problems. There is no point in being the best salesperson in the world if you do not get paid for your services. Far be it from me to be presumptuous enough to believe that I know all of the answers. I do not, and no one else does, either. The key, however, is to know most of the right questions. The answers ordinarily then become self-evident. The correct answer is often not as important as the correct question.

Knowledge is one of the keys to success. Good salespeople are successful because they take the time and effort to become intimately familiar with the products they are selling as well as the customers' problems and requirements. You should use those same principles in understanding and dealing with the relationship with your employer or principal.

Keep in mind that most salespeople have commission problems because of great success and not because of great failure. I have seen very few problems between sales representatives and their principals/employers which were the result of underperformance by the sales representatives. Most problems occur because the sales representative substantially exceeds expectations. It can sometimes help in dealing with the problem to recognize that your commission problem is a validation of your skills as a salesperson.

Notwithstanding all of the preceding chapters on the possible pitfalls in a relationship between a manufacturer's representative and his principal, or a sales representative and his employer, human relationships, both personal and professional, cannot always be organized and effectuated with mathematical precision and certainty. Interpersonal relationships are still based in large part upon trust, honor, and respect. Very seldom will you ever be able to negotiate the perfect sales representation agreement. You will never be able to eliminate all risk in anything you do. Normally the most we can hope for is to make the risks somewhat manageable. Remember that little risk generally means little reward.

There is always a possibility you will get burned in any relationship, personal or professional. If you give respect, honor, and loyalty, more often than not, it will be returned. If it is not, you may want to find someone else to work for.

Remember, when your working career is over, your success will not be measured strictly by the material possessions you have accumulated. It is not true that he who has the most toys when he dies wins. We are social creatures. We seek the respect, admiration, and love of our professional peers and family. Try to maintain a proper balance of economics, personal relationships, family, and friends. If you do, you will be a success!

ACKNOWLEDGMENTS

I would like to acknowledge and thank the following persons:

First of all, my wife, Susan Ludington Gillary, for her love and support during almost thirty years of marriage. Sue has never complained about the time and effort that was necessary for me to put into my work. She is my best friend, companion, lover, and a great mother to our four wonderful daughters.

My father, Jack E. Gillary, whom we lost in 1992. He taught me about business and life in the best way possible: by setting a good example.

My secretary, Mrs. Patricia Miracola, for her help, hard work, and loyalty for over fifteen years. I have had countless compliments from my clients over the years about her pleasant personality and helpfulness. She is generally the initial contact person for my office and she always makes a good impression.

Kevin Albus, my associate. Since joining my firm in 1995, Kevin has done most of the behind-the-scenes work while I get most of the glory. Kevin is a tireless worker and a great asset.

Dr. J. Harold Ellens, the former interim minister at our church. Dr. Ellens provided valuable insight and editing services. He has authored more than sixty-eight books and articles and is one of the most intelligent people I have ever met.

My oldest daughter Emily. She has done most of the work in preparing my first book for self-publication. Emily made sure that we took the right steps at the right time. I'd better also thank my daughters Jennifer and Katie because if I don't mention them, I will be in trouble. I love my daughters with all my heart.

I would also like to thank all of my clients over the past twenty-four years who thought enough of me to entrust their legal problems to me. I will always try to honor that trust.

ARTICLES BY RANDALL J. GILLARY

"The Three Stages in the Life of a Manufacturer's
Representative Agreement",
published in *Agency Sales Magazine* of the
Manufacturer's Agents National Association (MANA),
March, 1995

"The History of the Procuring Cause Doctrine in
Michigan",
published in *Michigan Bar Journal*,
December 1995

"What to Do When Your Principal Doesn't Pay Your
Commission",
published in *Agency Sales Magazine*,
April 1996

"Should Your Sales Agreement Contain a Mandatory
Arbitration Clause?"
published in *Agency Sales Magazine*,
December 1996

"Are You Sure You Are Being Paid the Proper Amount
of Commission?"
published in *Agency Sales Magazine*,
August 1997

"Eliminating Conflict of Interest Problems for
Manufacturers' Representatives",
published in *Agency Sales Magazine*,

December 1997
"Renegotiating Commissions",
published in *Agency Sales Magazine*,
August 1999

"The Michigan Sales Representative Commission Act
Revisited–Again or Does 'Intentionally' Mean 'In Bad
Faith'?"
Co-authored with associate Kevin P. Albus
2001 L. REV. M.S.U.-D.C.L. 965

"Providing an Incentive for the Sales Force"
published in *Agency Sales Magazine*,
March 2002